THE COMPLETE GUIDE TO

BUYING YOUR FIRST HOME

Roadmap to a
Successful, Worry-Free Closing

R. DODGE WOODSON

BETTERWAY PUBLICATIONS, INC.
WHITE HALL, VIRGINIA

Published by Betterway Publications, Inc.
P.O. Box 219
Crozet, VA 22932
(804) 823-5661

Cover design and photograph by Susan Riley
Typography by Blackhawk Typesetting

Library of Congress Cataloging-in-Publication Data

Woodson, R. Dodge (Roger Dodge)
   The complete guide to buying your first home:
 roadmap to a successful, worry-free closing / R. Dodge Woodson.
    p. cm.
   Includes index.
   ISBN 1-55870-228-8 : $14.95
   1. House buying. 2. Real estate business. I. Title.
HD1379.W66 1992
643'.12—dc20
                                                          91-42569
                                                              CIP

Printed in the United States of America
0 9 8 7 6 5 4 3 2 1

This book is dedicated to my daughter, Afton Amber Woodson,
and her mother, Kimberley W. Woodson.
Their unending support makes putting together a project like this enjoyable.
My parents, Maralou and Woody Woodson, deserve credit too;
they put me on the right track in life.
Thank you all.

Contents

Introduction

Welcome to the wonderful world of real estate. This book is intended to help anyone wishing to buy a home, but it is especially geared to first-time buyers. As a real estate broker and builder, I know what first-time buyers are up against when trying to buy that elusive first home.

My many years of experience in real estate will benefit anyone seeking a home. First-time buyers need special help and often run into unique problems. My book will guide you along the path to happy home ownership. As a first-time buyer, you will encounter numerous obstacles; this book will show you how to avoid the pitfalls and traps. It will also help you discover how to get the most for your money.

Purchasing real estate can be challenging for anyone and at times nearly impossible for the first-time buyer. Banks may not want to work with you if VA eligibility is a factor. Brokers may have little interest in the commission earned from a starter home. These are just two reasons buying your first home can be discouraging. By heeding the advice in this book, you can overcome the most common stumbling blocks to acquiring a home of your own.

I have done my best to make sure the information included in this book is accurate and complete, but books can become outdated quickly. Successful books have long shelf lives and may outlive the information contained in them. At this writing, all information is current and correct, to the best of my knowledge.

For your own protection, before making any decisions involving money or legal matters, consult a professional. Thank you! I hope you learn from and enjoy this book.

1
How Much House Can You Afford?

When you consider the purchase of your first home, the process can be overwhelming. Many people are willing to help you make a decision, but how will you know who is right? Family members and friends will get involved. They will base many of their suggestions on the real estate market of years past. If you follow their advice, you may not take advantage of current market conditions. Real estate brokers set up shop on every corner, trying to get you to buy your first home from them. These professionals will inundate you with advice, but how valid will it be? Brokers generally work for the seller and gain financially from your purchase. How far can you trust the advice of someone in that position?

Your friends will want to help you. They will recommend certain brokerage firms and condemn others. All of a sudden, everyone you know is an authority on what you should do. It is flattering that everyone wants to help, but you must draw a line to keep your sanity. When the dust settles, you are the one responsible for making the new monthly payments. You will be living in the house. The property and the terms should meet first and foremost with your approval. If your family and friends approve, that's fine, but first come *your* needs and desires.

There are many decisions to be made when you want to buy your first home. Many of these decisions are a matter of personal taste, but one isn't: how much house you can afford. If you are planning to finance part of your purchase, you will be subject to loan qualification rules.

There is little you can do about loan qualification ratios. You can become knowledgeable about various loans and coordinate your purchase with the most advantageous loan for your purposes. This is about as far as your control goes in the financing decision. If you are particularly creative, you may be able to stretch the rules a bit, but don't count on it. Since your entire purchase is riding on the financing, this seems a logical place to start planning.

If you are unable to secure financing, what style house you want is irrelevant. Financing is a critical issue in the purchase of most homes. As a first-time home buyer, you may have some hurdles to clear in your quest for financing. Consider the down payment, points, closing costs, and other expenses. How much will all this cost? Well, that depends on the type of loan and the lender. Financing can be manipulated when you know what to do and where to do it. Chapter 11 provides all the details you need to know about financing. This chapter will help you to determine your personal comfort level when it comes to mortgage payments.

Before you can judge your borrowing power, you must know what type of loan is best for you. The number and range of different loans intimidate some buyers, don't let this happen to you. Shopping for the right loan requires a lot of telephone work, but it will be well worth it. When you make the right loan choice, you can extend the loan amount you qualify for, reduce the down payment, or meet other personal desires. It is fairly easy to determine what the bank will say you can afford. This chapter is meant to examine areas of affordability not covered by a lender's loan ratios. For strict financing guidelines, refer to Chapter 11. Some of the terms in this chapter may seem strange at first. If you need clarification of a word or phrase, refer to the glossary in the back of the book.

GOING TO THE BANK

Lender ratios often project a monthly payment the average home buyer does not find comfortable. While ratios are meant to provide a reasonable estimate of the monthly payments you can afford, they can be deceiving. Ratios are based on averages; it is up to *you* to determine how much house *you* can comfortably afford. Loan ratios can influence different types of buyers very differently.

One buyer feels he can afford more than the lender's ratios will approve. Another buyer feels uncomfortable with a payment as high as that shown by the ratios. When you feel you can afford more than the amount supported by ratios, you have little to decide. The financial institution bases the loan approval process on the ratios. Except in rare cases, you will not be approved for a loan with payments exceeding an amount established by standard loan criteria. This part of the affordability puzzle is not hard to understand. You may not agree with the lender's policy, but if the lender says no, there isn't much you can do.

UNACCOUNTED FOR FINANCIAL FACTORS

When a loan officer qualifies you, he does not consider your special interests. He is only concerned with your financial obligations, not your financial desires. It is important to note that not all desires are hobbies or unjustifiable expenses. If you pay your own life and health insurance premiums, you know they can amount to a large monthly payment. The loan officer will not consider this bill when he qualifies you. Car insurance is expensive and is generally considered a necessity. Even so, the loan officer will not factor this expense into your qualification figures. Adequate insurance certainly

cannot be considered a frivolous expense, but it doesn't come into play in a lender's qualifying ratios. If you overlook this fact, you can fall into too much debt very quickly.

It is natural to assume the loan officer will not allow you to borrow more than you can repay. While this is a logical assumption, there are many occasions when it is false. It is your responsibility to determine how much you can comfortably afford to pay for your monthly house payment. How can you determine how much house you can afford? Many people have no idea how to establish a realistic monthly budget.

Today's consumer would rather not see how much money is spent every month. The idea is, "If you can charge it, you can afford it." That's like saying your checking account can't be overdrawn because you still have checks in the checkbook. If you are mature enough to buy your first home, you should be mature enough to establish a household budget. This is not as simple as some people might think.

ESTABLISHING YOUR MONTHLY EXPENSES

To develop a feasible budget, you must have an idea of what your monthly expenses are. Some individuals will make a budget in only a few minutes. They will sit down and list every monthly obligation that comes to mind. When this simple task is done, they will consider their budget projections complete. A few people will only jot down the expenses they hope to incur on a monthly basis. Neither of these methods will work. Before you can draft an accurate budget, you must accurately identify your present spending habits.

Again, some people will say, "Easy!" They will contend that all they have to do is jot down their monthly expenses from their checkbooks. They assume that this process will give an accurate rendering of current expenses. Do you believe that if you list all your checks for the last month, you know what your monthly expenses are? If you believe this to be true, reconsider your opinion! Think about it. How often do you buy lunch or gas or other items with cash? Your cash expenses are only one reason this approach will not prove accurate. How often do you pay your car insurance? Unless you paid the insurance in the month you listed the checks for, this expense will not show up.

Other hidden but routine expenses include: holiday gifts, vacations, illness, clothes, personal-property taxes, license-plate renewals, and countless others. These out-of-sight, out-of-mind expenses will haunt you if they are not accounted for. It is crucial for you to design a realistic budget before buying a home. If you don't, you could be forced into a very uncomfortable lifestyle. Big house, small purse. Now that you see some of the hidden expenses of your monthly budget, let's explore the concept further.

BUDGET COMPONENTS

The following information will assist you in outlining a realistic budget. It is hard to think of all your expenses without something to prompt your memory. These paragraphs will blaze a trail for you to follow in filling out your monthly budget. After reading these reminders, refer to the forms in the back of this chapter. The first form for establishing your budget is labeled, Present Monthly Expenses. You should complete this form with all your current spending habits. The second form is Proposed Monthly Expenses. Fill in this form with your future budget goals. Review each form and arrive at a monthly budget you feel is accurate. If you cheat, you are only hurting yourself. Now, read on to see what expenses you may be overlooking.

Rent

Your present rent is a fair barometer for establishing how much you would be comfortable paying as a monthly house payment. There are two big differences between rent and a mortgage payment. If you find the rent hard to handle, you can move to a less expensive rental unit. Once you are committed to a mortgage, you must sell the property to get out from under the monthly payment. Income-tax advantages are many with home ownership. A portion of your monthly payment should be recovered in tax savings. The exact tax advantages and consequences

will vary from buyer to buyer. To determine how the potential savings will affect you, consult a tax expert.

When you evaluate your current rent, look at how long you have been paying your present amount. If it is less than a year, you should carefully assess your ability to pay the rent for an extended time. It is easy to look at a rent payment you have only been making for the last four months and to determine that you can afford it. You haven't lived there long enough for any hidden expenses to catch up with you. Don't base your entire decision on what you pay in rent; there are other factors to consider in a house payment.

When you are paying rent, you are not paying real estate taxes. These taxes can quickly amount to more than a hundred dollars each month. There are other expenses associated with owning your own home that you don't have to deal with in rental property. These expenses will be noted throughout the chapter.

The Electric Bill

This is an expense most people include in the first draft of their budget. It is a common expense that most people recognize and think about. If you live in an apartment where the utilities are included in your rent, you might not think of budgeting for an electricity expense. By comparing your rent in a utilities-included rental to a house payment, you could be setting yourself up for an unpleasant surprise. When you buy your own home, you have to make the utility payments.

If the house you buy has electric heat, the electric bill could devastate your budget. Even an electric water heater can make your monthly bill imposing. If you are not used to making these kinds of payments, be sure to allow for them in your homeowner's budget. If you neglect to budget for a $125 a month electric bill, where will you come up with the money?

Heating and Cooling Costs

Some landlords pay heating and cooling bills. If this expense is figured into your rent, you might not include it in your budget. Depending upon where you choose to live, these expenses could be the straws that break your financial back. If you are not accustomed to paying for these expenses, do some research. Ask your friends what their home heating and cooling expenses average through the year. Talk with utility companies to arrive at a fair estimate. Whatever you do, don't forget to include a figure for these expenses in your budget.

Telephone Expenses

This expense is one almost everyone is used to paying. As an everyday expense, you would think it would be easily remembered when drafting a budget. Yet some people will not think to include it in their monthly debt service. Another fact to consider is the location of your new home. Will you be in a different phone exchange and run up expensive long-distance bills to talk to family and friends? When you are charting your budget, every expense counts. Don't leave any cost unaccounted for.

Cable Television Service

If you plan to receive monthly cable service, you better plan on paying the bill. This expense may seem trivial, but it must be included in your budget. If you like, you can build two budgets. The first will include only the most important, routine expenses. The second will include luxury expenses, like cable television. Setting up two budgets can show you how much money you must have and how much you would like to have.

An expense such as cable television is not a need. It is a desire and may stand between you and your first home. Only you know what you are willing to do without to obtain a home of your own. Using the two-budget method will show you both angles of your buying power. While you may not be willing to sacrifice certain expenditures, at least you will know what they are. This information can help you in determining how much house payment is too much.

Health Insurance

For some people, health insurance is a company benefit provided by their employer. For others, it is a sizable monthly expense to be reckoned with. If you pay your own premiums, include them in your budget. The same is true of dental insurance. If you have to pay for it, it has to go into the budget.

Many insurance fees are paid on a quarterly basis. This can make them difficult to remember. Since they are not a monthly entry in your checkbook, they can be passed over without acknowledgment.

Medical Expenses

How much do you spend each year for medical expenses? These expenses include doctors' fees, dentists' bills, and medication. Look back through your records and derive a monthly figure for your medical expenses.

If you have children, you can count on regular medical bills. For the average family of three, a monthly figure of $35 is the least you should carry in your budget. This amount will be affected by the type of insurance you have, but don't omit medical expenses from your budget. They are difficult to project, but they come when you least expect them.

Life Insurance

If you have limited life insurance now, you should consider increasing it when you buy a home. It will be hard enough on your spouse to lose you, but if the spouse loses the home too, it will be even worse. When you are young, life insurance may seem like a waste of money, but as you mature, it becomes more valuable. When you become indebted for a mortgage, the importance of life insurance rises dramatically. Do you want to leave your partner with a house payment that has taken two incomes to meet? Face the fact: you should include a life insurance figure in your homeowner's budget.

To project accurate insurance costs, contact several insurance agents for quotes. Explain your plans and ask for their advice. Never jump at the first proposal put in front of you. Insurance is a very competitive field, and you must work to determine the best deal for you. Keep in mind that not all insurance agencies offer the same products. Shop until you feel comfortable with the product and the agent; then, use the premium cost as your budgeting figure.

Car Payments

Here is an expense you are not likely to overlook. If you have car payments, include them in your budget. If your car is paid for, how long do you believe it will last? After answering this question, you may want to budget for new car payments in the near future. For the average person, owning a car is a necessity. To earn an income, you must be able to get to work. Unless you live in a large city, this means owning a vehicle.

To keep your job, you must maintain reliable transportation. Many first-time buyers don't think about having to replace their paid-for car. When they look at their monthly expenses, they never factor in a car payment. This isn't hard to understand if their present vehicle is paid for. Yet when that car must be replaced, they are in trouble.

If these buyers invest all their money in a home, how will they pay for a replacement car? For most, their only option will be to finance it. This creates a monthly payment that was not figured into the budget. Adding a car payment to your financial needs can be quite a strain. Consider your transportation situation carefully when projecting a budget. If you expect to replace your car soon, allow for the down payment and monthly payments in your budget. If you plan to pay cash for your replacement transportation, allow for this figure in your home-buying calculations.

Auto Insurance

Car insurance is a fact of life. While you may hate it, you must continue to pay for it. The cost of insurance is not something you want to overlook when building your budget. Many auto policies require premium payments on a quarterly or semi-annual basis. When the expense is not a monthly one, it is easily overlooked. Auto insurance can add up to more than $600 a year very easily. A hidden expense of this magnitude can make a major impact on your lifestyle. If you neglect to include this expense in your budget, you may be walking to work.

Gas, Car Repairs, and Maintenance

Since most of us drive our cars, we need fuel for them. If you use a credit card for your gas purchases, you may remember to include the cost of transportation in your figures. If you pay cash, this expense may go unnoticed in your budget. Don't forget to include fuel expenses in your projections. When projecting these costs, allow for the location of your new home. Will your gas expenses increase with the new location?

If you own a vehicle, you must invest money in it each year. It may only be for tuneups and oil changes, but you must spend money on your car. Check your past history and compile a monthly figure to represent these expenses. Take a look at your tires — when will they need to be replaced? Buying new tires can cramp your style if you are on a tight budget. It is best to allow for unforeseen expenses when you project your budget. If you don't, you can get into deep financial trouble before you know it.

Water and Sewer Expenses

This is a category most tenants never pay directly. Typically, the landlord pays water and sewer usage fees. As a homeowner, if you have municipal water and sewer services, you will be responsible for the bill. If you buy a home with a well and septic system, you will still have expenses. The well pump uses electricity every time it pumps water. The septic tank must be pumped periodically. All these costs must be included in your budget.

Mail Service

Will mail be delivered to your new home or will you need to rent a postal-service box? This may be a small expense, but it is still an expense. Another consideration is your annual postage expense. What does it cost you to mail all your letters and bill payments? Think about these expenses when putting together your projected annual costs. This may seem to be going overboard, but the more costs you define in your budget, the less likely you are to get into financial trouble.

Food

Here is an expense that is universal and mandatory. Without food, a house won't matter because you will not last very long. Computing your food expense may be difficult. It is not enough to look only at what is spent in grocery stores. You must allow for all food and beverage expenses incurred during the year. This includes: restaurants, soft drinks, fast-food lunches, snacks, and every other type of food-related expense.

When you reflect on your monthly food expenses, you may decide to go on a strict diet or an extended fast. Food-related expenses account for a major portion of most family's monthly expenses. When I was working on my budget, I tracked my cash outlay for food over several months. I must admit that the amount spent on food-related items was much higher than I would have guessed. There is nothing that can make you face reality like an accurate spreadsheet. I suggest you take a long look at what you spend to feed your family. The results will surprise you.

In addition to food, allow for other staples in the household. Detergent, toothpaste, paper towels, and other similar items can really add up. Since you may not buy these items on a monthly basis, you must go back several months to project an accurate budget.

Vice Money

If you smoke or drink, you could be spending a substantial amount of unrecognized money. You may not like facing the facts, but look at what you have spent in the last few months on vices. Many of my clients are unwilling to admit how much they spend on these items. They seem to believe if they don't know how much their vices cost, they will not have to alter their habits.

I have worked with people who spent more than $150 a month for cigarettes and liquor. I am not recommending that you change your habits; that choice is up to you. But you must acknowledge the expense of your indulgence. It is easy to fall into expensive habits. If you order pizza every Friday night, you are a victim of habit. This simple habit can easily cost you $40 a month. Don't fall into the trap of swearing off all vices to afford your new house. If you can drop the bad habits, that's great, but don't base your budget on changing your lifestyle dramatically and overnight.

Old habits are hard to break. If you plan your new-house budget based on giving up long-time habits, you may be miserable. Chances are, you will have trouble breaking the habits. It will be frustrating. When you couple those feelings with straining to make your house payment, you won't be a very happy homeowner.

School Costs

Whether you are pursuing continuing education or have a child in school, education expenses add up fast. Perform a complete accounting of these costs and project them for the future. Education is important, and it should receive consideration in your home-buying decision. With the ever-increasing cost of education, you could find yourself trapped.

As your career progresses, you may want additional schooling. Without continuing education, your job may be at risk. You wouldn't be the first person to be pushed out of a job because of an outdated education. If you feel you may be limited by your academic standing, it is wise to allow for additional educational expenses in your budget.

Child Care

The cost of full-time child care has reached deep into the pockets of many parents. Child-care costs can rival the earnings from a full-time job. If you are depending on the income from two careers to finance your home, think about the expense of child care. With some jobs, the cost of day care devours most of the paycheck. Even if you don't have a child, this may be an expense you will incur in the not-too-distant future.

For couples just starting out, a high mortgage payment can affect their family plans. The cost of rearing a child is one of the largest expenses a young family has. It is easy to say you can live on love, but love will not make the mortgage payment. If children are a factor in your life, don't underestimate the money needed to care for them.

Personal Property Taxes

Personal property taxes are not usually at the top of your list, but they can cost hundreds of dollars each year. Check your past records and include the cost of these taxes in your budget. These taxes are usually levied against cars, boats, trailers, and other high-ticket personal items.

Club Dues

Are you a member of the local fitness club? Do you shoot skeet at the club on weekends? If you enjoy the benefits of a club membership, include the fee in your monthly cost projections. A few rounds of golf and club dues could rival your real estate taxes. It could also prevent you from being able to pay the expenses of home ownership.

Professional License Renewals

If you hold a professional license, you probably have to renew it regularly. Whether you are a licensed plumber or a real estate broker, you must keep your license active. This may not amount to much money on a monthly basis, but you have to account for the cost in your projections.

Holiday and Other Gift Expenses

Gift giving can be very expensive. Christmas is an expensive holiday for many families. If you give gifts at Christmas, build a figure into your budget for this annual expense. Do you enjoy going away for long weekends when holidays roll around? With the high cost of travel and lodging, you cannot afford to take these costs for granted.

When you are a member of a large family, birthday gifts can be a noticeable expense. Consider what you normally spend on birthdays, and add the figure to your list.

Clothing

The cost of clothing varies with each individual, but it exists for all of us. When you must present a high-fashion image for your job, the cost of clothes can stretch into thousands of dollars. For the average family, the cost will be less, but you must compute the monthly cost in your projections. Since clothing is often not considered as a monthly expense, it can be easily forgotten. If you don't leave enough room in the budget for clothing, you may be very embarrassed walking down the street.

Charitable Contributions

Depending upon your beliefs, church contributions can be a routine expense. Buying cookies from your local Scout troop may be a standard expense. If you take pride in your efforts to help worthy causes, allow for them in your budget.

Hobbies

Hobbies can be extremely expensive. Buying your own home will not end your desire to pursue your favorite hobby. The list of high-dollar hobbies is too large to detail, but you know what you like to do and you should know how much it costs. When you develop your monthly spending needs, include a reasonable amount to indulge in your personal escapes and private pleasures.

Vacations

Vacations may be only an occasional expense. You may feel a big vacation is mandatory. Look at what you are used to spending, and allow for vacation money in your budget. There is no reason to strap yourself with such high house payments that you cannot take a break from time to time.

TOTALING IT ALL UP

By using the forms in the back of this chapter, you can now build an accurate budget. The work you do in this early stage will make you better prepared to make an intelligent and realistic buying decision. It is critical for you not to become enthralled with the projections of an aggressive loan originator. While it is important to work with your lender to establish your maximum loan amount, it is more important to determine the amount with which you are comfortable.

Once the papers are signed, you alone make the payments. If the payments are too high, your loan originator will not offer any comfort. He will not say, "Skip the next payment and enjoy your annual vacation." Once you make a loan commitment, you must make the payments. Chapter 11 will show you the banker's opinion of what you can afford. It is up to you to use the information in this chapter to determine the amount *you* feel is affordable.

PRESENT MONTHLY EXPENSES

ITEM	MONTHLY EXPENSE	ITEM	MONTHLY EXPENSE
Rent/House payment	_____	Life insurance	_____
Electric bill	_____	Disability insurance	_____
Heating bill	_____	Dental insurance	_____
Phone bill	_____	Tenant/Homeowner insurance	_____
Car payments	_____	Professional license renewal fees	_____
Car insurance	_____	Business expenses	_____
Car maintenance	_____	Personal property taxes	_____
Gas expense	_____	Personal grooming expenses (haircuts, etc.)	_____
Cable television	_____	Club dues	_____
Trash pickup	_____	Gifts	_____
Lawn care	_____	Vacation expenses	_____
Snow removal	_____	Personal savings plan contributions	_____
Water & sewer expenses	_____	Professional fees (accountants, etc.)	_____
Housing maintenance	_____	Medical expenses	_____
Food	_____	Dental expenses	_____
Clothing	_____	Pet expenses	_____
Child care	_____	Credit card bills	_____
Bad habits	_____	Installment loan payments	_____
Hobbies	_____	Other:	_____
Family entertainment	_____	Other:	_____
Educational expenses	_____	Other:	_____
Child support	_____	Subtotal (B)	_____
Alimony	_____	Subtotal (A)	_____
Health insurance	_____		
Subtotal (A)	_____		

TOTAL ESTIMATED MONTHLY EXPENSES _____

PROPOSED MONTHLY EXPENSES

ITEM	MONTHLY EXPENSE	ITEM	MONTHLY EXPENSE
House payment	_____	Life insurance	_____
Electric bill	_____	Disability insurance	_____
Heating bill	_____	Dental insurance	_____
Phone bill	_____	Tenant/Homeowner insurance	_____
Car payments	_____	Professional license renewal fees	_____
Car insurance	_____	Business expenses	_____
Car maintenance	_____	Personal property taxes	_____
Gas expense	_____	Personal grooming expenses (haircuts, etc.)	_____
Cable television	_____	Club dues	_____
Trash pickup	_____	Gifts	_____
Lawn care	_____	Vacation expenses	_____
Snow removal	_____	Personal savings plan contributions	_____
Water & sewer expenses	_____	Professional fees (accountants, etc.)	_____
Housing maintenance	_____	Medical expenses	_____
Food	_____	Dental expenses	_____
Clothing	_____	Pet expenses	_____
Child care	_____	Credit card bills	_____
Bad habits	_____	Installment loan payments	_____
Hobbies	_____	Other:	_____
Family entertainment	_____	Other:	_____
Educational expenses	_____	Other:	_____
Child support	_____	**Subtotal (B)**	_____
Alimony	_____	**Subtotal (A)**	_____
Health insurance	_____		
Subtotal (A)	_____		

TOTAL ESTIMATED MONTHLY EXPENSES _____

2
Defining Your Needs and Desires

Before you can buy your first house, you must determine what you are looking for in a home. In casual conversation, describing your requirements may be easy. When the time actually comes to make a long-term financial commitment, your criteria may be more difficult to define. It is easy to say you want a fireplace, but are you willing and able to pay an additional $3,800 to have it? Defining the essential features of your first home becomes much more difficult when dollar signs are placed beside the attributes of the home.

Most first-time buyers must work with a limited budget and minimal resources for a down payment. You need to be realistic about what you need and what you can afford. If you set your sights too high, you will remain a tenant for years. Many people keep saving and saving until they can afford a special feature, such as a garage. Your attempts to save enough to have everything you want in a home cannot keep up with real estate appreciation and inflation. Many people assume that because it took them years to afford their first house, it will be years before they can buy a subsequent home. This flawed thinking leads them to look for the perfect first home.

Few first properties can, or do, meet all the buyer's criteria. The restrictions of limited financial resources associated with first-time buyers often make the dream of obtaining their home a nightmare. When you remove the mystique from the purchase, you will often find your first home is just a stepping stone to a bigger and better house. For this reason, you can justify going without extras. On the other hand, buying a house that does not meet your basic needs is a costly mistake. What can you do?

Before you can begin your search for a home, you must know how much house you can afford. Chapter 1 showed you how to establish your budget and how to determine your financial strength. Now that you know how much you can spend for a home, it is time to see what you can get for the money. Buying your first home is an exciting proposition, but one frequently plagued with frustrating side effects. You must not allow elation to blind you when it comes to assessing your needs. Neither should you give in to confusion and settle for less than the best deal available.

It is not mandatory to forgo the features you feel strongly about in a house. It is, however, necessary for you to separate preference from necessity. As an experienced real estate broker, I have helped many people buy their first homes. My knowledge will enable you to purchase the best house you can afford. After years of working with first-time buyers, I know the types of questions and problems you will be faced with. Armed with some essential skills and basic information, you will be able to jump off the tenant treadmill.

Convincing yourself to buy a two-bedroom home could be a major mistake. You are less likely to be satisfied with the cramped conditions, and trying to sell the home can be extremely difficult. Housing markets are unpredictable, so don't assume you will be able to sell your home easily and move up to a bigger one. Whenever feasible, try to buy a home with at least three bedrooms. Selling a three-bedroom home is much easier and more profitable than selling a two-bedroom house.

If your budget prohibits the purchase of a three-bedroom home, look at smaller homes with expansion possibilities. The expansion options could include converting attic space into living space, finishing part of the basement, or building an addition onto the house. Pay attention to the characteristics of a prospective home's land area and restrictions. Be sure you are able to add space later, if the need arises.

Ideally, a home should have a least one and a half bathrooms. As more and more couples have two working partners, additional bathroom space increasingly becomes a need. Spouses should not have to battle for the use of a bathroom. Multiple bathrooms eliminate this friction. In homes with more than three bedrooms, there should be a minimum of two full bathrooms. A powder room or half-bath, in addition to the two full baths, is an excellent selling point and convenience.

COMPROMISE

Wanting a house with a huge country kitchen is no reason to continue renting. Your *desires* may initially appear to be *needs*, causing you to give up your search before it has begun. Many people assume they will never be able to find a house with all the qualities they want. This will be true if you are not realistic about your requirements and your financial abilities. Be willing to compromise, but don't become frustrated and buy the first home you can afford. Walking the thin line of compromise is an arduous journey. It is easy to become disenchanted when seeking the ideal home. After weeks of seeing homes you like but cannot afford, you may be easily swayed into settling for just a house. This one factor prevents vast numbers of prospective home buyers from fulfilling their dreams.

If you do not adequately define your buying criteria, this unsettling phenomenon is much more likely to occur. One of the most common mistakes of first-time buyers is to tour properties on the market in order to determine what they want in a home. This frequently results in impetuous buying. The visual impact of seeing attractive features assembled in one property can convince you it is the home of your dreams. This makes it easy to fall in love with a house that is beyond your financial reach. If you become infatuated with a specific house, it will be extremely hard to accept anything less. Setting guidelines and rules for your search, *before you start looking at properties*, is the most effective way to avoid this dilemma. Strictly adhere to the criteria you establish, and don't even look at houses outside your buying power.

FINDING JUST THE RIGHT HOUSE

Is it possible for first-time buyers to obtain just the right house? There is no reason you should give up on owning your own home. Depending on your financial capabilities and personal tastes, the task may be difficult, but not impossible. There are many ways to stretch your buying power, but these methods are worthless if you cannot decide what to buy. The first step is to sequester your emotions and deal with the decision on a strictly analytical basis.

Make a List

A good starting point in this process is to list your desires and minimum requirements. If you must have three bedrooms, it is senseless to consider homes with only two bedrooms. Looking at a wide range of houses will only confuse you. Inspecting homes beyond your purchasing capabilities will disappoint you and taint the remainder of available properties. Making accurate lists of your needs and desires will relieve you of these burdens.

Making lists may sound like a ludicrous waste of time. Yet you will be amazed at the hours of indecision and frustration this simple exercise will save you. I am speaking from *experience*. Before showing properties to buyers, I insist they make these lists. It saves both of us time and aggravation.

There are two forms at the back of this chapter: Basic Personal Housing Needs and Basic Personal Housing Desires. These forms list the most common needs and desires of first-time home buyers. Circle the items that pertain to you. Once completed, the information will give you a clear illustration of the items you should consider before viewing potential properties.

Feel free to expand on the lists. The purpose is to simplify your individual decision-making process and to narrow the field of suitable homes. When you ponder the number of bedrooms required, consider these factors. Are you likely to expand your family in the next five years? If you anticipate a growing family, try to find a home with an additional bedroom or suitable expansion potential. Effective needs evaluation should take this type of future requirement into consideration.

When completing the form containing your compulsory needs, be thorough and realistic. A full basement or in-ground swimming pool is rarely a need. Concentrate on basic design and construction features. How many bathrooms must you have? One generally meets the need, but an additional half-bath is always desirable. Would you consider a dishwasher, garbage disposer, or whirlpool tub a necessity? Under average conditions, these items fall into the desire category.

An efficient heating and cooling system should be included on your list of needs. Safe electrical wiring definitely belongs on the list of requirements. A properly functioning plumbing system and a roof that doesn't leak should be listed among your needs. Having a living room and a family room is nice but not a necessity for suitable shelter. Formal dining rooms don't rate as needs, and garages should be considered luxury items. Adequate insulation is a requirement and energy-efficient windows and doors may be requirements.

Use Common Sense

The key to this phase of defining your housing needs is common sense. If you can do without a feature without undue hardship, it is not a need.

Place items in this category on the list of desired features. If you are fortunate, you will still be able to obtain some of these items in your acquisition. They will give you something to work towards and keep your home-buying endeavor exciting. You will get a great sense of accomplishment from purchasing a house that meets your needs, accommodates your budget, and appeases your desires as well. The lists will guide you towards successful, effective home buying.

SETTING THE STYLE

Once you have established your basic needs, follow similar procedures to determine the best style of home for you. Two-story houses often offer the most habitable space for your investment. These homes are traditionally less expensive to build and buy. When your preference points to a home without stairs, a ranch-style home is the best choice. You may prefer to compromise with a split-level home. This style of home is cost effective when built on the proper site, and it has fewer steps than a traditional two-story home.

Cape Cod designs are perfect for the first-time buyer with limited financial resources and the prospect of a growing family. Cape Cods lend themselves to economical expansion and a low, entry-level sales price. Many of these homes are built with the first-time buyer in mind. They are constructed with suitable living facilities on the first level and an easily expandable, unfinished upstairs. Capes are great grow-as-you-go homes.

Other styles include saltbox homes, split-foyers, contemporary houses, and solar designs. Property descriptions will include colonial, farm, traditional, English Tudor, French Provincial, and Spanish construction homes. Exterior styles are accentuated with various roof designs. These roof variations include gable, hip, flat, shed, mansard, gambrel, and gable with dormers. In most cases, house styles are a matter of taste and are not part of housing needs.

These fashion terms may not mean much to you, but a home's style has a direct relation to its value.

Before seeking the perfect home, decide what style home meets with your approval. The more specific your requirements are, the more likely you are to find and acquire the proper home. Eliminating some houses with checklists and concentrated thought before beginning your search will make your home-buying experience easier and more enjoyable. Complete the form called Style and Construction to fine-tune your housing preferences. This form can be found at the end of the chapter.

STRUCTURAL SAVINGS

Are you willing to live in a house built on a concrete slab, or do you require a full basement? The cost difference between these construction methods is wide. If a basement is not necessary, homes built on slabs and crawlspaces will save you money. The difference can amount to thousands of dollars. This type of savings can make the difference between being able to buy a property and just looking at it.

For example, the savings difference of a basement vs. a crawlspace could easily exceed the amount of money needed to pay your closing costs. How important is it for you to have a home with a garage? When you are able to get by without a garage, your savings could make your down payment. If the home is situated on a suitable lot, a garage can be added later, when your finances are stronger. Interior features, like entrance foyers, add elegance to a home, but they also increase the sales price. Depending upon design, the cost may be negligible, but any savings can make the difference in getting your first home. Mud rooms are another example of a desire. Certainly, you can live without a mud room. By eliminating this desire, you may save enough to furnish several rooms in your new house.

Do you feel you must have a formal dining room? Most first-time buyers can survive without a separate dining area. Eat-in kitchens are popular and keep your acquisitions costs lower. The same is true of formal living rooms and family rooms. When monthly payments and overall price are serious factors, eliminating the formal living room makes sense. Although you might enjoy the formal space, it is unlikely that you need it. Hardwood floors,

fireplaces, tiled showers, and wainscoting are all attractive, but these accents to a home are expensive desires. None is a necessity, and they can push a home out of your affordability index.‑

Is a cedar shake roof worth the extra cost? There is little justification for paying for an expensive roof on your first home. Asphalt shingles will keep you just as dry, and they cost much less. The aesthetic value may not be as great, but as long as you have your own roof over your head, it doesn't have to be an expensive one. This may seem like a minor consideration, but every little extra expense diminishes your ability to buy your first home.

APPLIANCES

Appliances should be accounted for in your decision-making guidelines. Once you buy your home, the need to furnish it with appliances can be a sobering experience. Look through a few catalogs and add up the cost of new appliances. Price a refrigerator, range, washer, and clothes dryer. These items are essential appliances and will cost upwards of $2,000. If you fail to include these necessities in your housing-purchase budget, you will be in for a rude awakening.

Most houses on the real estate market are equipped with a range and a refrigerator. Washers and dryers are less likely to be included in the sales price. When you negotiate on your home, try to have all appliances included in the purchase price. Appliances are considered personal property, also known as chattel, and are not required to be included in the sale of a home. As you walk through a home, don't assume the appliances you see are included in the sales price.

When you reach the offer stage, Chapter 12 will help you be sure the appliances are part of the offer. Unless you include the appliances as a defined element of your offer, you may not get them. Your need may suddenly become an expensive option. The cost of adding an item can determine whether it is a requirement or a desire. If you do not have the extra money to buy a range, make sure you put this appliance on your needs list. One of the major reasons for defining your needs is to ensure that they are included in the property you buy.

WINDOW TREATMENTS

Window treatments are another consideration in establishing your housing budget and needs. As with appliances, it is natural to assume drapes, blinds, and curtains you see on the walk-through are a part of the deal. These items are also chattel and may not be included in the advertised sales price. In some homes, especially solar homes, purchasing specialty window treatments can be very costly. Make certain you have a clear understanding as to the ownership of anything you consider a need.

LOT SIZE

Lot size is another factor in ascertaining your minimum requirements. How much land is enough? Evaluate your needs and plans for the real estate surrounding your new home. Buying more land than you need will cost more at the time of purchase and in subsequent years, in the form of property taxes. Wanting a home situated in the middle of forty secluded acres is a fine fantasy, but it may not be practical for your first purchase. Take some time to think about your land requirements and record your findings on the list of needs. These details will be helpful when placing priorities on potential homes.

AIR CONDITIONING

Depending upon location, air conditioning may be mandatory. To some folks, air conditioning is extravagant. Yet in some areas of the country, a home's market value can be adversely affected if the home does not have air conditioning. Health factors are also a consideration. If you suffer from allergies or bronchial ailments, air conditioning may be a necessity. This type of evaluation is important in your home-buying decision.

SPECIAL NEEDS

Some people have special needs not included in the forms at the end of the chapter. The lists are based on common public needs and desires. They may not match your personal requirements, but they will give you a sense of direction in defining your purchasing parameters. Individuals with physical restrictions may have needs that are not mentioned on the lists provided. The same could apply to people with large families or pets. Don't take these lists as the last word in needs and desires. They are not intended to relieve you from the responsibility of compiling your own personal data. Their intent is to guide you in the right direction with your conclusions.

DON'T CUT IT TOO THIN

Although it is important to eliminate superfluous features, like garages and decks, be careful not to reduce your needs to the ridiculous. When establishing your bottom line, you may determine you could manage to live in a small home with only two bedrooms. Chances are, you could make concessions and find a way to survive, but this should not make buying a two-bedroom home a prerequisite. Just as style affects value, so do other basic elements. Dwellings with only two bedrooms are less expensive, but they appeal to a much smaller segment of the buying public when you attempt to sell the house later.

When you trim features to save money, consider resale value. Many novice home buyers make the mistake of eliminating the wrong features. Frequently, they believe their first house will later become their retirement home. This is rarely true. Houses are seldom kept for twenty or thirty years, until they are paid for. The average property owner will sell and relocate in less than ten years. In many parts of the country, these moves are made in three to five years. In Chapter 6, you will learn why cutting too many corners can be detrimental to the future return on your investment. The need to recover your investment quickly, say in the case of military families, can be significant.

Even if you are sure you will never move, the statistics indicate that you will. Don't force yourself to wait until you can afford the perfect house to begin your home ownership. It is unlikely that you will ever be able to satisfy all your housing goals in a first home. The keystone to years of happy home ownership is acquiring that elusive first house. Once you take title to your private real estate haven, your ability to move up to a more desirable home increases dramatically.

CONTROL YOUR IMPULSES

Defining your needs and controlling your impulses to look beyond them will protect you from coveting what you cannot have. Once your buying criteria are established, you are ready to begin looking for your new home. When reading advertisements, you should rule out houses that don't meet your specifications. Looking beyond your means will only result in disappointment and resentment. Seeing houses with qualities that conflict with your pre-determined plans will confuse you. These problems are unnecessary and will reduce your enthusiasm and desire to become a homeowner.

Buying your first home is a special occasion. There can only be one first home in your life. The entire process should be exciting and joyous, but all too often, it results in frustration. By following a few simple steps, such as making lists, you can limit the risk of disillusionment. Don't ignore the importance of developing a viable plan for purchasing the right home for your needs.

It may seem cruel to set your desires aside for a few years and to wait, but in the end, it can be the deciding factor in successful real estate procurement. Properly assessing your needs will enable you to purchase an appropriate first home. This home will unlock the benefits of home ownership now and open the doorway to more luxurious properties in the future.

BASIC PERSONAL HOUSING <u>NEEDS</u>

LAND _____

Front Lawn:

❑ large   ❑ medium

❑ small   ❑ fenced

Rear Lawn:

❑ large   ❑ medium

❑ small   ❑ fenced

❑ Road frontage

❑ Proper building lot drainage

STRUCTURE _____

❑ Watertight roofing

❑ Sound structural integrity

❑ Wood frame construction

❑ Solid foundation

❑ No known defects in construction

❑ Standard ceiling heights

SYSTEMS AND INSULATION _____

❑ Adequate water and sewer service

❑ Efficient and reliable air conditioning (regional)

❑ Efficient and reliable heating system

❑ Efficient and reliable plumbing system

SYSTEMS AND INSULATION _____

❑ Plenty of hot water

❑ Strong water pressure

❑ Efficient and reliable electrical system

❑ Minimum of 100 amp circuit breaker electrical service

❑ Adequate lighting

❑ Adequate insulation

❑ Proper foundation ventilation for crawlspaces

❑ Proper attic ventilation

❑ No water or moisture problems

DESIGN _____

❑ Adequate living space

❑ Eat-in kitchen or dining area

❑ Minimum of two bedrooms

❑ All appliances included

❑ Vinyl floor covering in baths and kitchen

❑ Adequate kitchen cabinet and counter space

❑ Minimum of one bathroom with tub/shower combination

❑ Carpet floor covering except for baths and kitchen

BASIC PERSONAL HOUSING <u>DESIRES</u>

LAND _____

❏ Side lawns

❏ Attractive landscaping

❏ Level topography

❏ Large building lot area

❏ Low real estate taxes

❏ Underground utilities

❏ Uniform building lot shape

❏ Restrictive covenants

STRUCTURE _____

❏ Brick foundation

❏ Gutters and downspouts

❏ Brick construction

❏ Solar construction

❏ Maintenance-free exterior (i.e., vinyl siding)

SYSTEMS AND INSULATION _____

❏ Energy-efficient windows and doors

❏ Public water and sewer connections

❏ Wood stove or wood stove hook-up

❏ Central vacuum system

❏ Well-lighted kitchen

DESIGN _____

❏ Porches

❏ Decks

❏ Foyer

❏ Mud room

❏ Wallpaper

❏ Tile bathroom

❏ Fireplace

❏ Hardwood floors

❏ Formal living room

❏ Formal dining room

❏ Exterior storage

❏ Unfinished basement

❏ Expandability

❏ Third bedroom, or provisions for same

❏ Additional half or full bathroom

❏ Standard floor plan with good traffic patterns

❏ House style in keeping with neighborhood

❏ Exterior siding and color complemented by surrounding homes

❏ Walkway from parking area to front door

❏ Adequate parking for at least two cars

STYLE AND CONSTRUCTION

FOUNDATION _____

- ❑ Slab
- ❑ Pier foundation
- ❑ Crawlspace
- ❑ Full basement
- ❑ Concrete foundation
- ❑ Parged cinderblock foundation
- ❑ Brick foundation
- ❑ Stone foundation

STYLE _____

- ❑ Ranch
- ❑ One story
- ❑ One and one-half story
- ❑ Saltbox
- ❑ Cape Cod
- ❑ Two story
- ❑ Split foyer
- ❑ Split level
- ❑ Solar
- ❑ Earthen
- ❑ Log home
- ❑ Farm house
- ❑ Colonial

STYLE _____

- ❑ Traditional
- ❑ Spanish
- ❑ English Tudor
- ❑ Contemporary
- ❑ French Provincial

SIDING _____

- ❑ Masonite
- ❑ Vinyl
- ❑ Aluminum
- ❑ Wood clapboard
- ❑ Cedar shake

ROOF _____

- ❑ Cedar shake
- ❑ Asphalt shingle
- ❑ Flat
- ❑ Shed
- ❑ Hip
- ❑ Gable
- ❑ Mansard
- ❑ Gambrel
- ❑ Gable with shed dormer
- ❑ Gable with window dormer

3
Building vs. Buying

When people dream of owning their own home, the dreams often focus on having a custom home built for them. The fantasy revolves around having the perfect home constructed to meet your personal specifications. Many first-time buyers dismiss this idea after talking with a builder and reviewing the additional expenses incurred in building a custom home. Having a home built is frequently much more expensive than buying an existing house. While this is often the case, it is not always true. Before giving up on your dream home, you owe it to yourself to explore all the possibilities.

When you begin to shop for your first home, you will be faced with many choices. There are many pre-owned homes to choose from. Previously owned homes may offer the most home for your investment dollar. These houses will be accompanied by new homes built on speculation. Houses built on speculation are often found in new subdivisions. If you are looking for a rural setting, a spec house can be hard to locate. Subdivision homes are known in the industry as tract homes. Tract homes are usually very similar in their construction and features.

Tract builders will generally offer three models to choose from. The three models could be a one-story ranch home, a two-story colonial, and a one-and-a-half story Cape Cod. These model homes will offer the promise of a new home, but your personal influence will be restricted.

Custom builders are willing to create your dream. They will work with your ideas to build the perfect home. With some courage, you can contract for the building of your own home. This task requires personal effort and research, but the savings can be enormous.

Finally, if you are qualified, you might build your own home. You must assess each of these possibilities to arrive at the best decision.

A CONFUSED MIND ALWAYS SAYS NO

Faced with so many possible opportunities, many first-time buyers are unable to make a decision. There are so many possibilities you may become confused and frustrated. There is a saying in the sales business: "A confused mind always says no." This observation is very true. When you are confused, it is easier to give up than to pursue your fantasy. If you fall into this category, you may be a tenant for a very long time. There is no reason to be intimidated by your choices. Organizing and evaluating your needs and desires will answer the majority of your questions and calm your fears.

Chapter 2 defined the difference between needs and desires. In this chapter, you will get an idea of how to determine the best type of housing to meet your goals. Some individuals will buy an existing home. Some will work to purchase a new tract home. Others will venture into the unknown and have a home built to their liking. A few will use their abilities and become an integral part of the construction of their home to get more house for the money. None of these decisions is wrong. The final decision must be based on your needs and abilities. What follows is a blueprint for determining the best buying decision for your situation.

EXISTING PROPERTIES

Existing homes comprise much of the first-home buyer's market. In most areas, there is an abundance of previously owned residences, and prices are typically more affordable than for other forms of housing. These two factors place existing homes high on a first-time buyer's priority list. Among these properties are single-family homes, condominiums, co-ops, and small multi-family properties.

The potential advantages to small multi-family buildings are numerous; Chapter 8 details them. Homes needing renovation are another possibility when considering existing properties. This group of properties requires careful consideration. Buying "handyman specials" will be fully explored in Chapter 4. For now, we will concentrate on ready-to-move-into homes and new-construction homes.

The most common lure to existing homes is their price. Because they are not new or custom built, the price is usually lower. Another motivating factor of these properties is the buyer's ability to see what he is buying. When you plan to have a home built new, you must *imagine* what the finished product will be like. New construction often requires you to pick your house from blueprints, or even to design it yourself. While this freedom is an advantage to some buyers, others want to see first-hand what they are buying. Existing homes provide a sense of security and reality.

PRICE DOES NOT ALWAYS REFLECT VALUE

Just because an existing home is less expensive than a new one does not mean that it is a better deal. A low price could indicate a property with problems. Maybe the basement leaks or the heating system needs to be replaced. In older homes, the plumbing could be deteriorated, requiring a large cash investment to repair. Remember, a low price is usually low for a reason. Chapter 6 will help you to identify problems and teach you what to look for in a home.

For comparison, assume that the properties discussed here are in good condition. What are the other advantages of buying a used home? One advantage is you are likely to see what the neighborhood is like. When building, you may not know what the other properties around yours will be like. Existing homes have established lawns and landscaping. These advantages are something you will not have for a while with a new home. A used home will have settled; if the walls or ceilings are going to crack, you will discover it in your inspection. In a new home, it can take over a year for little problems to pop up.

Another plus: you will know what the property taxes are for an existing house. With new construction, the taxes are projected but unknown. If you are buying an existing condo or co-op, you will have historical data to review. This information accurately indicates the fees associated with ownership of these units. In a new project, the fees charged by the property owner's association could fluctuate rapidly after the first year. If the project is established, you will have a good idea of the annual increases in the association fees.

NEW VS. OLD

Buying a previously owned property should cost less than buying or building a new home. Someone else has lived in the home, and the price will reflect this fact. The walls may be dirty and the carpet could be worn; these factors dictate a lower asking price. Many older homes do not offer the features of new homes. They may not be as energy-efficient; this difference could mandate a lower price. All in all, existing houses should be the least expensive of your options.

TRACT HOUSING

When buying a new tract home, you may be able to see a model home before committing to a contract. Builders and developers of large subdivisions frequently provide models for prospective buyers to evaluate. While a model is representative of the home you may buy, it is not the precise home for which you contracted. The fear of buying something they cannot see is strong in some buyers.

A big advantage to a new home is the warranty. A one-year warranty is standard, but many builders offer a ten-year warranty. Where warranties are concerned, buying a home can be compared to buying a car. When you buy a used car, the warranty is limited and the risks are great. When you buy a new car, you are protected by a comprehensive warranty for many miles and years to come. The same rule applies to houses. If you buy an existing house, who is responsible for replacing the worn-out furnace? In most cases, if the furnace dies after you close on the house, it is your problem. With a new home, it is the builder's responsibility. Warranties on new homes make their higher price easier to justify.

The time span between signing a contract and moving in is another difference to consider. If you contract to buy an existing home, you could be living in it in sixty days. With a new home, it could take twice as long, or longer, before you can move in. If you are on a tight timetable, new construction can pose problems. Brand new homes and existing homes offer advantages and disadvantages.

BUILDING A NEW HOME

While most people are somewhat aware of what to expect with existing homes, they are frequently confused by the requirements and demands of new-home construction. It is only natural for first-time buyers to be curious about building their own home. If owning your own home is the American Dream, having your own home built, or building it yourself, is the Great American Dream. As a builder, a real estate broker, and a seventeen-year veteran of the housing industry, I am going to clear up your confusion about building.

There are two basic approaches to obtaining a newly-constructed, custom-built home. You can hire a builder to build it for you or you can build it yourself. This may sound like a simple choice, but it is not. Deciding to build the home yourself can take on several meanings. Will you physically build the house? Will you act as general contractor and hire independent subcontractors to construct the

home for you? Will you do a little of both? What do you mean when you talk of building your own home? These are only the first questions to be answered in your decision to build a house.

Hiring a Builder

If you plan to hire a builder, how will you find a reputable one? Will you choose from the builder's portfolio of plans or will you have your home custom designed? Who will supply the construction financing — you or the builder? Will the builder require your permanent loan to be approved before construction is begun? Will you be able to lock in your permanent loan for a long enough period to have the home built? All of a sudden, a simple decision to build your first home is getting complicated. This is the point where many would-be buyers give up the idea of building.

These questions are all real, and they must be answered. Finding the right answers is important, but it does not have to be overwhelming. There are many ways to obtain a custom-built home; one of them should suit you and your situation. The process of sorting through the possibilities will take time, but much of it will be fun. To begin unraveling the mystic shroud of building a home from the ground up, let's start with hiring a builder.

The first consideration in hiring a builder is the task of finding a suitable one. Not all builders are alike; spend enough time to find the best builder for your home. A builder accustomed to building $300,000 homes will not be the best choice for a starter home. Most contractors in this class will not be willing to build an affordable home. They know builder profit is directly related to the appraised value of a home. The more the home is appraised for, the higher the builder's profit. Building contractors base their earnings on a percentage of the home's value. You would be reasonable to expect a builder's gross profit to be 20% of the appraised value.

Building upper-end custom homes takes time. Six months to a year is not an unreasonable period of time to allow for a luxurious home. The intricate trim and finishes in more expensive homes require extra time. Some builders prefer to work with starter homes. They can complete them in less than three months and move on to another project. Matching the builder to your style of home is an important element in the building process.

Checking Your Builder Out

Once you have selected a few builders, you should check them out. Use the Builder Information Sheet in the back of the chapter to gather information on the prospective contractors. Go to homes they are building and inspect the work. Call their references and see if the customers are satisfied with their homes. Check with the codes enforcement office and the state licensing agencies. Confirm the contractor's information given on the Builder Information Sheet. Verifying the contractor's credit references will tell you a lot about the builder. When you are sure your builders are reputable, proceed to the next stage.

Picking a Plan

The next step is to decide what you want to build. This part can be difficult and fun at the same time. Chapter 1 taught you how to determine what you can afford to pay for a house. Now, you must see how much you can get for your money. With the help of Chapter 2, you know which features are essential and which are luxuries. Keep the two types of features separate and in perspective. The first objective is to own your own home; the goodies, like a garage or a pool, can come later.

Essential Features

Before sitting down with the builder, make a list of items you want in the house. Do you want a dishwasher? How important is it to have a family room and a living room? Use the checklist of Essential Features at the back of the chapter to determine what your home must contain. As you go through the checklist, make a separate list of items you would like to have but are willing to live without. The form called The Wish List will give you a place to jot down these notes; you can find it also at the back of the chapter.

Make a Specification Sheet

With these lists complete, you are ready to make your specification sheet. The specification sheet will help you get accurate bids from your general contractors. List all the features you want included in the house on the spec sheet. Now, you must determine what type of house will be built to these specifications.

Do you want the home to have a basement, a crawlspace, or a slab foundation? What type of roof design do you like? Will the home have two stories, or will it be all on one level? Your builders will be able to advise you on the pros and cons of different building techniques.

Where Do You Want the House?

When you know what type of home you want, you must decide where you want it. Do you want an in-town lot or rural acreage? This part of the decision should be easy; you know where you would prefer to live. When you narrow down the types of locations you will accept, you are ready to meet with some builders. You have completed a very good package for the builders to work with. You know the type of lot you want, the house style, and the main features. With this information, the builders will be able to provide you with the remaining information you need.

Arrange a Meeting

Arrange a private meeting with each of your selected builders. Ideally, you should meet with at least three contractors. At the meeting, give the builder a copy of the specifications and ideas you have created. Ask for each builder's opinion on your proposed plans. Trust me: you will get a different response from each builder. They will all have their personal opinions; remember them. This is valuable feedback. When the builders talk, you should take notes for future reference.

Experienced contractors can provide you with price-less information. You may not agree with all of it, but you should pay attention to each builder's comments. When you are at home, you can go over your notes and evaluate the suggestions. This stage of the building process is critical. This is where you are fine-tuning your dream home. Don't let a builder push you into something you don't agree with. Wait until you have the opinions of all the builders to make a decision on what you should and should not build.

Getting a Price

After you have refined your building plans, ask each builder to give you a price for the same job. The plans and specifications you provide to each builder must be identical. If they vary, so will each builder's price. When you opt to hire a general contractor, you only have to be concerned with getting one price from each general contractor. If you act as your own general contractor, this part of the venture is dramatically different. We will get into these differences a little later. For now, all you have to do is compare the quote packages received from each builder.

Look for the Hook

When you get their proposals, read each one carefully. Be certain each builder is bidding the job with the same plans and specs. Some builders use substitution clauses to outmaneuver their competitors. A substitution clause could look like this: "Heating system to be a 125,000 BTU, gas-fired boiler, manufactured by XYZ company, or equal." If you see something like this, don't allow the builder to get away with it. Substituting materials can save the builder money and cause you disappointment and problems. Make all bidders work with the same products and plans.

When you have all your prices in, double-check them for accuracy. Be sure they correspond to your request and do not exclude anything. Some builders hide behind exclusions. They may state that their price is subject to price increases. This gives them the opportunity to raise their price at will. An exclusion clause could exclude site work. Site work might account for 10% of the total cost to build the house. If a builder excludes it, his price is going to beat the competition. Beware of these ploys to dazzle you with a falsely low bid.

Choosing Your Builder

When you are comfortable with the prices, you must choose a builder. Use the Builder Profile Form in the back of the chapter to rate the builders. By answering the questions on the Builder Profile Form, you can judge each builder fairly. With this done, enter your personal feelings about the contractor at the bottom of the form. Using facts and common sense, you will be able to choose a competent builder.

Let's review what you have accomplished to this point. So far, you have completed these steps:

- Decided to hire a builder
- Matched selected builders to your type of house
- Defined essential features
- Created a wish list
- Made a specifications sheet
- Determined what style home you want
- Decided on the location
- Received prices from several builders to do the job
- Evaluated the builders
- Chosen a builder

With all this done, you are well on your way to having a custom home built. Most of the drudgery is done, and the fun still lies ahead. What should you do next?

The Paperwork

The next step is to complete formal paperwork with the builder you have chosen to construct the home. With the exact location chosen and plans and specifications complete, you are ready to talk contract. Many builders will have a standard contract. If you are willing to accept a builder's contract, have it examined by your attorney before signing it. It may be in your best interest to have your attorney prepare a contract for the job. Most contracts favor the individual supplying them. When you work with a builder's contract, you are normally in the weaker position. A reputable builder will not hesitate to sign a reasonable contract prepared by your attorney.

Contract Clauses

The wording in the contract is very important. There should be clauses in the contract to protect you against common problems with new construction. These clauses should include specific wording. Some of the clauses needed are:

- A date construction will be started.
- A date construction will be complete.
- A penalty clause for each day the home is not finished after the completion date.
- A closing date.
- Detailed provisions for how your earnest-money deposit will be handled.
- A contingency clause allowing you to break the contract if you are unable to obtain the type of financing you specify in the contract.

The list of items could continue for many pages. An experienced real estate attorney will be able to provide you with a comprehensive contract. Spending money to have a thorough contract prepared is one of your best investments. When problems arise with new construction, it is frequently the result of a poor contract.

Digging the Hole

When the contract is signed, you must seek financing. When your loan is approved, the general contractor can begin building. This is an exciting time in your life. Every day you will see changes being made to the raw land you chose to build on. When you first see the footings for the home, you may be terrified. The footings always look much smaller than they are. Many people see the footings and are convinced the builder is making the house too small. Even after measuring the footings, it may be hard for you to believe they are the correct size. This optical illusion will change once the floor and exterior walls are built.

Following the Progress

As the construction progresses, you will see your dream becoming a reality. Having hired a builder, all you have to do is to enjoy the building of your new home. After a few months, the home will be complete. When the builder has obtained a certificate of occupancy, you need to complete a punch list. The punch list is composed of minor repairs and adjustments the builder must make before transferring the home to you. You inspect the property, making a list of all the items requiring attention. Once the home meets with your approval, you will be ready to close your loan and take ownership of the property. With your homeowner's insurance purchased, you will sit down at the closing table. In less than an hour, the new home is yours.

When done systematically, having a new home built is not a horror show. It can be a lot of fun and very satisfying. The comfort of having a new home with a good warranty will offset the additional cost associated with a new home. If you have the time to wait for a home to be built, you can have the features you want, in the home you desire. If money is a problem, there are alternatives.

Money Matters

Down payments and monthly payments have much to do with the homes an individual considers. Even with existing homes, the down payment can be a high obstacle to hurdle. It is not easy to save enough money to make the required down payment. While you are saving money, real estate prices are going up. Every year you save, appreciation requires you to save more. This can get very frustrating. There are ways to work around this problem. One way is to take a very active interest in the building of your new home.

Being Your Own General Contractor

Even if you don't have the skills to build the home physically, you can learn to be your own general contractor. Acting in this capacity should save you more than enough money to offset the down payment requirement. The money you save by being the general contractor can be used as sweat equity. Not all lenders will accept this form of down payment, but some will. If this is what you want to do, start by talking with financial institutions.

Sweat equity is value you earn in the property by performing work yourself to lower construction costs. When banks loan mortgage money, they base the loan amount on a percentage of value. This is called the loan-to-value (LTV) ratio. If a bank requires a 10% down payment, they are making a 90% LTV loan. By acting as your own general contractor, you should save between 10% and 20% of the home's appraised value. This savings puts your loan request within the guidelines of the LTV requirements. With a liberal lender, this is all the down payment you will need.

If you do some of the physical work yourself, the savings will be much more. Something as simple as cleaning up after construction can save several hundred dollars. Any effort you put forth to reduce construction costs can be translated into the down payment. While this principle works in theory, it is a little more difficult to structure in real life. Banks have taken some heavy losses in real estate loans. By nature, they are nervous and will want proof that you can fulfill your promise.

If you have no experience in any construction-related business, you could have a hard time making a sweat-equity deal. The lender will be apprehensive of your ability to perform the duties of a general contractor competently. While you are likely to meet with some resistance, the potential benefits of sweat equity are well worth pursuing. Don't give up if you are turned down by the first few banks. Examine the reasons each bank refused your loan and refine your presentation for new lenders. With persistence, the odds are good you can strike a deal with someone.

If you act as the general contractor, you will be responsible for the entire construction procedure. This is not a job to be taken lightly. You will need ample time to oversee and coordinate the building process. If you have a full-time job, you must have the flexibility to make daytime phone calls. You should also be prepared to work late into the evening. Scheduling subcontractors, ordering materials, and inspecting the work are only part of what you will have to do. The money you save will be well earned.

Hit the Books

Building your own home without the help of a professional builder is quite an undertaking. There is not enough space in this book to explain all of the requirements. If this is an angle you would like to pursue, take the time to read books dedicated to the subject of contracting your own home. One such book is *The Complete Guide to Contracting Your Home* (2nd edition, Betterway Publications, Inc., 1992).

Many other respected publishers offer similar books. If you read these books, you will get an idea of what will be expected of you. Sweat equity is a powerful tool when you learn to use it. By studying and being persistent, you can gain the ability to make your fantasies come to life.

The decision of building versus buying an existing home is a complex question. There are many advantages to each side of the decision. The ultimate choice will be determined by you and your abilities. A compromise is possible. Buying an existing home in move-in condition is one good choice. Building a new home, or having one built, is another option. One compromise may be to purchase a property needing renovations. This option allows you to use sweat equity without starting from scratch. You will have an existing structure to work with and improve upon. The next chapter explains the opportunities presented by fixer-uppers.

BUILDER INFORMATION SHEET

Name: _____

Principal's Name: _____

Address: _____

Phone Number: _____

JOB REFERENCES

Job One: _____

Job Two: _____

Job Three: _____

CREDIT REFERENCES

1: _____

2: _____

3: _____

Bank: _____

Licensed? _____ Insured? _____ Bonded? _____

How long in business? _____

Any complaints filed in the last five years? _____

How long is the warranty period on the house? _____

COMMENTS

Price _____ References _____ Appearance _____

REMARKS

ESSENTIAL FEATURES

FEATURE   **COMMENTS**

Location   _____

Lot Size   _____

Lawn Area   _____

Style   _____

Type of Foundation   _____

Type of Siding   _____

Type of Roof and Roofing Materials   _____

Type of Exterior Windows and Doors   _____

Garage   _____

Paved Parking Area   _____

Public Utilities   _____

Type of Heating and Cooling Systems   _____

Insulation   _____

Hardwood Floors   _____

Carpet   _____

Vinyl Flooring   _____

Stairways (Wood or Carpet)   _____

Wallpaper   _____

Interior Doors and Trim   _____

Closets and Storage Space   _____

Fireplace   _____

Wood Stove or Hook-up   _____

Kitchen Size   _____

Appliances   _____

Dining Room   _____

Living Room   _____

Family Room   _____

Den/Study   _____

Number of Bedrooms   _____

Size of Bedrooms   _____

Number of Bathrooms   _____

Spa or Whirlpool Tub   _____

Mud Room   _____

Laundry Room   _____

Decks   _____

Porches   _____

Expansion Potential   _____

Real Estate Taxes   _____

THE WISH LIST

FEATURE	COMMENTS
Location	_____
Lot Size	_____
Lawn Area	_____
Style	_____
Type of Foundation	_____
Type of Siding	_____
Type of Roof and Roofing Materials	_____
Type of Exterior Windows and Doors	_____
Garage	_____
Paved Parking Area	_____
Public Utilities	_____
Type of Heating and Cooling Systems	_____
Insulation	_____
Hardwood Floors	_____
Carpet	_____
Vinyl Flooring	_____
Stairways (Wood or Carpet)	_____
Wallpaper	_____
Interior Doors and Trim	_____
Closets and Storage Space	_____
Fireplace	_____
Wood Stove or Hook-up	_____
Kitchen Size	_____
Appliances	_____
Dining Room	_____
Living Room	_____
Family Room	_____
Den/Study	_____
Number of Bedrooms	_____
Size of Bedrooms	_____
Number of Bathrooms	_____
Spa or Whirlpool Tub	_____
Mud Room	_____
Laundry Room	_____
Decks	_____
Porches	_____
Expansion Potential	_____
Real Estate Taxes	_____

BUILDER PROFILE

NAME: _____

CATEGORY	POOR	FAIR	GOOD	EXCELLENT
Price	❏	❏	❏	❏
Promptness	❏	❏	❏	❏
Professionalism	❏	❏	❏	❏
Helpfulness	❏	❏	❏	❏
Licensed	❏	❏	❏	❏
Insured	❏	❏	❏	❏
Bonded	❏	❏	❏	❏
Experience	❏	❏	❏	❏
General Knowledge	❏	❏	❏	❏
Credit References	❏	❏	❏	❏
Job References	❏	❏	❏	❏
Honesty	❏	❏	❏	❏
Phone Response Time	❏	❏	❏	❏
Thoroughness in Bid	❏	❏	❏	❏
Time in Business	❏	❏	❏	❏
Feelings toward Builder	❏	❏	❏	❏

COMMENTS

4
Fixer-Uppers, Are They for You?

How many times have you seen advertisements for handyman specials in the newspapers? These ads are always intriguing, but you have to wonder how much is wrong with the home. How much money could you save by purchasing the property and making the repairs yourself? Fixer-uppers are in a category all their own. The cost of renovations varies with each property. Some will make excellent investments; others will give you nothing but grief. As a first-time buyer, should you consider buying a house needing renovation? There is no clear-cut answer to this question. First-time buyers can be as different as the properties they purchase. This chapter will show you both sides of the Great Fixer-Upper Debate.

WHO IS RIGHT?

Buying a home with known defects seems stupid to some people. They will contend there is no viable reason to spend good money on a house needing immediate work. People on the other side of the debate will argue their position to the end. They believe buying and remodeling a rundown home is an excellent idea. Part of their reasoning is based on development of sweat equity. They know that the potential exists to make big money from rehabbing an old house. Which group would you tend to side with? After reading this chapter, you will be educated in the options available through handyman specials. Your opinion, from either side of the debate, could take a 180 degree turn after you read this section of the book.

THE PERFECT SOLUTION?

Buying a fixer-upper is the perfect solution for some first-time buyers. If you are mechanically inclined or can act as your own general contractor, you can build equity in the property fast. With a good loan-request proposal, you may be able to buy the home without a cash down payment. Many lenders will make an acquisition and arrange for an improvement loan for properties in need of renovation. Frequently, these loans will be made with the loan amount based on the value of the property *when the renovations are complete*.

Typically, you will supply the financial institution with a detailed set of plans and specifications for the proposed improvements. The lender will ask an appraiser to develop an appraisal using your plans and specs. The appraiser will inspect the existing home and envision how your rehab work will improve its value. The appraiser will then provide a report on the anticipated value of the completed project. The lender may then approve a loan for up to 80% of that amount.

The loan officer will advance the money needed to purchase the property as part of the acquisition loan. Then, as work is completed, the lender will reimburse you at periodic intervals for completed work. This procedure will continue until the work is complete, up to the 80% amount. When the job is done, you will have a 20% equity in the property. At that time, you may be able to refinance the home for a loan up to 95% of the appraised value. This is a good way to get into a house without a cash down payment, if you are capable of doing the job.

Acting as your own general contractor, your efforts will be worth about 20% of the renovations done. If you do some of the physical work, your equity position will be even stronger. If you are careful in planning your improvements, the money you invest in renovations will increase the home's value significantly. Knowing which improvements to make will strongly affect the final value of the property.

WHAT TO DO?

Some improvements are much more valuable than others. If you convert the attic into living space, you have made a wise choice for appraisal purposes. Finishing an underground basement is generally not a good move when working with appraised values. The completed value will reflect little more than your investment for finishing the basement. Remodeling the kitchen and bathroom will have a positive effect on the appraisal. Replacing the roof will not help your equity much, unless the existing roof is worn out. New carpet will make the property more appealing, but it will not inflate the appraisal much above your improvement cost.

The first secret to making money with fixer-uppers is knowing which improvements to make. The second secret is knowing how to choose a good property for rehabilitation. The third trick is knowing how to act as your own general contractor. The last element needed to be successful with rehab property is an ability to work the appraisal and the financing. I am going to give you two examples. The first is the wrong way to handle a fixer-upper. The second is the correct method for making a handyman special work for you.

THE WRONG WAY TO DO IT

Joe Handyman sees an ad in the paper for a handyman special. The advertisement describes a house with the basic features he wants. According to the ad, the house is in need of major work, but most of it is cosmetic. He makes an appointment and sees the house. On the first tour, the house appears to

have potential. After thinking about the house overnight, he calls and makes arrangements for a more thorough inspection.

For the second inspection, Joe takes two of his friends along to check out the house. His two buddies work in construction; one is a painter and the other is a new-construction carpenter. The three go through the house, inspecting it room by room. As they inspect the home, Joe's imagination runs wild with possibilities for improvements. After the inspection, he talks the project over with his friends.

His plans are made, and he gets the house under contract. Careful research has trained Joe in how to set up the financing. The lender has agreed to loan 80% of the home's appraised value. The loan will be based on the property value after improvements are made. The appraiser asks for a detailed set of plans and specs. Once the appraiser reviews the proposal, an appraisal report is issued to the bank. Joe receives a commitment letter in the mail, stating the terms of the loan for which he qualified.

The letter requires Joe to provide a 5% cash down payment, in addition to acting as general contractor. Joe has the money for the down payment and agrees to the terms. It is his intention to refinance the home when the repairs and remodeling are complete. His construction buddies agree to help with the rehab work. When all the paperwork is complete, Joe closes on the property. Finally, he owns the house and can begin the work.

Joe begins the job with enthusiasm as the general contractor. According to the plans, he will be building a large amount of equity in the property with his improvements. As he gets into the job, problems crop up. The exterior walls are not insulated. The crawlspace under the house has standing water in it. The old electrical wiring constantly blows fuses. After using the plumbing, Joe discovers that the pipes drain very slowly. A plumber tells him the old galvanized pipes have closed up and must be replaced. All these problems were not anticipated; at least, not by Joe and his friends.

Joe tells the bank about the unexpected problems, but they offer little help. They maintain their position in loaning only the agreed upon amount of money. Joe turns to his parents for help. They are sympathetic and loan additional money for the mandatory repairs. Breathing a little easier, he continues with the planned renovations. Fortunately, there are no more bad surprises during the rehab work.

When Joe has finished all the work, the bank sends the appraiser to inspect the work and confirm the completed value. In a few days, he receives a letter from the bank with a copy of the appraisal. He is confused about the appraised value. Joe purchased the rundown house for $60,000. The rehab work cost $23,000. The total investment is $83,000, and the house is appraised for only $89,000. Joe is sure the appraiser must have made a mistake. A phone call to the appraiser ruins his day; there is no mistake. The house is only worth $89,000.

The bank agreed to loan a total of 75% of the appraised value, $66,750. Joe had planned on making a 5% down payment. Combining the 5% down payment with the bank loan equals $71,200. This leaves him with $11,800 invested in the home that the bank will not finance. Much of this is the money borrowed from his parents. How will he pay them back? What went wrong with the deal?

By refinancing the home with a 95% loan, Joe is able to borrow $84,550. He repays the first bank loan and his parents. After paying off these two loans, he has $1,550 left over. Because of loan fees and closing costs, he must reach into savings to satisfy all the financial demands. When the dust settles, Joe has earned less than $3,500 for his time and effort. He did get a house without a cash down payment, but he invested many hours of his time. In the end, he was able to get a home without a down payment, but he could have done much better.

The Mistakes He Made

This buyer made many mistakes. The first mistake was in the inspection of the property. The house had many underlying problems a professional inspector would have discovered. The exterior wall insulation could have been checked by probing around the electrical outlets. By taking the outlet covers off, an experienced inspector would have discovered that there was no insulation in the walls. The standing water in the crawlspace could have been found if the buyer had looked for it. Many buyers never look under a home to inspect the property.

Crawlspaces can harbor many problems. They could be full of water or infested with termites. They may not be insulated. The floor structure could be rotted. The buyer should have crawled under the home before purchasing it. Testing all the plumbing fixtures would have shown the drain defects. This would have been a simple act, but the buyer neglected to do it. By inspecting the wiring and electrical panel, the buyer might have been suspicious of the old wiring. A professional inspector would have known from the beginning whether the wiring was adequate and safe.

The buyer made another big mistake in the improvements made to the home. He should have consulted with an appraiser before making the improvements. He made superfluous improvements instead of equity-gaining changes. Repainting the exterior only to change the color was a waste of money. The original paint was in good condition, so the appraiser did not increase the value because of the new paint job. A brown house is just as valuable as a white one. All the money spent on mandatory repairs was lost. The appraiser would not give much value to the appraisal for making these repairs. If the buyer had installed new plumbing fixtures, he would have seen an equity gain. Replacing old pipes will not do much for the appraised value.

Another flaw in this rehabber's plan was taking too much for granted. He thought his equity gain would be in proportion to the money invested. In the end, he found this to be far from the truth. If he had paid for a before-and-after appraisal prior to purchasing the property, he would have known exactly what to expect from his improvements. The appraisal would have cost about $300, but the buyer would have been dealing with the facts. The handyman expected to refinance the finished product to extract cash profits for his efforts. In this example, there were few profits to extract. He owed the bank and his parents. All his Herculean efforts only added $6,000 of equity to the house.

THE RIGHT WAY TO DO IT

You see an ad in the paper for a handyman special. The advertisement describes a house with the basic features you want in a home. According to the ad, the house is in need of major work, but most of it is cosmetic. You make an appointment and go to see the house. On your first tour, the house appears to have potential. After thinking about the house overnight, you call and make arrangements for a more thorough inspection.

After your inspection, you make an offer to purchase the property with some contingencies in it. You reserve the right to have a professional home inspector inspect the house. If the results of the inspection do not meet with your approval, you may void the offer and have your earnest-money deposit returned. A second contingency allows you to void the deal if your research shows renovation costs to be out of proportion to the anticipated completed value of the property. The third contingency is tied to your ability to obtain suitable financing for the acquisition and renovation of the property. These contract provisions keep you in control and allow you a way out of the deal if it sours in the early stages. Always allow yourself an "escape hatch."

The inspector gives the property a clean bill of health regarding its structural and mechanical systems. The deficiencies in the property are proven to be only cosmetic. The lender is willing to provide suitable financing. Working with the appraiser, you have determined the present value of the property. It is worth every penny you are paying for it. In addition, you know precisely what effect your proposed improvements will have on the home's value when completed. With all these facts, you seal the deal and close on the property.

Following advice learned from extensive study, you coordinate the job and hire subcontractors for the technical work. Knowing your limitations, you perform all the work you are qualified to do. Instead of repainting the home, as in the first example, you have vinyl siding installed. Your remodeling includes the kitchen and bathroom. Instead of buying all new kitchen cabinets, you have the existing cabinets fitted with new doors and fronts. The old stained sink is replaced with a new stainless-steel sink. The bathroom is your second target. The torn vinyl flooring is replaced and the bathtub is resurfaced to give the appearance of a new tub. The wall-hung sink is replaced with a vanity and cultured marble top.

Your subcontractors build a closet in the den to convert it into a bedroom. Building a partition wall across the huge living room creates a separate family room. Your improvement dollars are spent wisely, and the home's value soars. When the job is complete, your total investment is $83,000. The appraiser comes for an inspection of the finished home. When you receive the appraisal report, the home is valued at $109,000.

THE DIFFERENCE

What made your rehab efforts worth $20,000 more than the first example? You installed vinyl siding to create a maintenance-free exterior. The work you did in the kitchen and bath was prudent and profitable. By converting the den into a bedroom, you gained significant equity. Dividing the existing living room into two rooms had a positive effect on the appraisal. You have played the rehab game very well. When you refinance the home with a 95% loan, your loan will be in the amount of $103,550. With $89,000 invested, your equity gain is $20,000.

You not only purchased the home without a cash down payment, you generated a respectable profit for your efforts. This outcome was not the result of luck. You approached the project with a plan *and* thorough research. Fixer-uppers offer the opportunity for dedicated individuals to make money while securing their first home.

KNOW WHAT YOU ARE GETTING INTO

If you are interested in pursuing fixer-uppers, you owe it to yourself to know what you are getting into. Rundown properties can provide you with a home and a profit. They can also cause you countless problems. To be successful renovating a neglected house, you have to pay your dues. The equity gain is not a free ride; you must earn the equity. Before jumping into a rehab project, investigate what will be required of you. This can be done by talking with contractors and reading books.

DO YOUR RESEARCH

There are numerous books available on the subject of remodeling houses. Reading will not only show you how to do the job, it will spark questions in your mind. When these questions arise, write them down. When you feel you have exhausted your study aids, consult with local professionals. Talk with appraisers and contractors. Your reading will provide a basic knowledge of the questions to ask. The research will also prepare you to understand the terminology used in the industry. If you are contemplating the purchase of a rehab project, you must prepare yourself for the challenge.

Many professional contractors are afraid to renovate existing properties. With new construction, it is much easier to estimate your costs. Dealing with existing conditions, you may come upon many unfavorable surprises. Unless you are a seasoned remodeler, tackling a rehab project will test your skills. While handyman specials are alluring, they can result in despair. It is critical for you to be well informed before taking this route to home ownership.

5
Real Estate Brokers

When you begin looking for a new home, you will almost certainly come into contact with real estate brokers. Looking through newspaper advertisements, you will discover that a majority of the properties are listed with brokers. As a buyer, you will most likely deal with real estate brokers in the purchase of your first home. It is important for you to understand your relationship with brokers. It is also helpful to know how brokers operate and what you can do to improve your buying position.

The real estate industry is surrounded by myths and misunderstandings. The public has limited knowledge of their rights and the laws pertaining to real estate brokers. When you are placing your future in the hands of a broker, you had better know what is going on. Brokers are professional salespeople and can influence your decisions. This power can be dangerous when in the wrong hands. A good broker is a treasure, but a bad one is a disaster.

You do not have to leave this critical stage of your buying decision to chance. With some background knowledge, you can protect yourself from bad brokers. Depending upon your qualifications, you may not need a broker, but most people benefit from the services of a reputable broker. There are advantages and disadvantages to working through a broker. These will be examined and explained throughout this chapter.

After determining their buying power, the next step for many prospective purchasers is to call a broker. This can spell disappointment from the start. Brokers are notorious for showing you properties at the upper limit of your price range. They anticipate you will extend your price ceiling to acquire the perfect home. When using a broker, few people spend *less* for a home than the maximum for which they qualify. This is not by coincidence. Most brokers are paid a percentage of the sales price. The more expensive the house, the more the broker pockets. Consequently, brokers tend to recommend more expensive properties. Remember, brokers are trained salespeople. If you have a concise definition of the home you are willing and able to buy, a broker's sales pressure will be ineffective.

I am not suggesting that you close your mind to a seasoned professional's opinion. Experienced brokers can provide you with valuable information. Their suggestions are often valid and in your best interests. I am advising you to set your own parameters and carefully sift through information provided by brokers and home sellers. It is imperative that you do not fall into the trap of impulse buying. Anyone with something to gain from your buying decision may give you biased advice.

If you plan to deal with brokers, you should learn how to choose a good one. Picking a broker at random from the phone book is not a good idea. It is also important to know whom the broker is really working for. When buyers walk into a real estate office, they assume the broker they talk to is working for them. This is rarely true. Most brokers work *with* buyers and *for* sellers. The fiduciary relationship of the broker must be established.

THE SELLER'S BROKER

One of the first professionals you are likely to run into is the seller's broker. The seller's broker is working for the seller, to sell the real estate. When the property is sold, the seller will pay the real estate commission. Normally, the primary goal of the broker is to sell the property quickly for the highest possible price.

The seller's broker must treat you fairly, but the broker's loyalty is to the seller. What will the broker do for the seller? She will perform many tasks in the quest for her commission. She will advertise the property and handle inquiries from the ad. She will qualify prospective purchasers before showing them the property. If the buyer is qualified, the broker will arrange to tour the seller's home. The broker should gather information about the purchaser at every opportunity.

She will attempt to make her probing questions seem like a friendly interest. While she may be genuine in her interest, she is collecting valuable information in her discussions with you. This personal information is stored for later use when the broker attempts to close the sale. After showing the property, she will ask you more questions. All these questions are designed to give the broker an edge in negotiations.

If you make an offer to purchase the property, the seller's broker will deliver the offer to the seller. She may write the offer for you if there is no other broker involved. If you have another broker or an attorney prepare your offer, the seller's broker will still deliver it to the seller. In most cases, the seller's broker will provide information and advice to aid the seller in making a decision about your offer to buy.

When the seller makes a decision, his broker will return the results of his decision to you or your broker. This could come in the form of a contract, a rejected offer, or a counter offer. If you come to terms with the seller, the broker will assume a new role. She has closed the sale on paper and will divert her energy to completing the transaction. This will involve acting as an overseer for the process that follows.

The seller's broker will work to keep the scheduled events on track and to update the seller on the progress toward closing. This may require the bro-

ker to make frequent phone calls and to arrange for inspections of the property. If you are having various inspections to remove contingencies, she will make herself available to meet the inspectors. It will be her responsibility to open the house for them and to monitor their activities for the seller.

When it is time for the appraisal, she will meet with the appraiser at the house. She may only serve to allow access to the appraiser, or she might provide information to the appraiser. If there is some doubt as to whether the house will be appraised high enough, she will provide evidence to support the agreed upon sales price.

Throughout the buying process, this broker will work to hold the deal together. She knows that if it falls apart, she will not be paid, and the seller will not be happy. The seller's broker may deliver paperwork, take water samples, or do any number of other tasks required to settle the sale. The broker will be ready to re-sell you on the home if it becomes necessary. It is not unusual for buyers to get cold feet following the acceptance of an offer.

If the broker senses that you are getting nervous, she will switch back to a sales mode. As a professional broker, I have had to re-sell the buyer as many as three times in sixty days. If the road to closing is rocky, buyers get frustrated. The seller's broker must be prepared for this and make the buyer comfortable again.

The seller's broker may be instrumental in providing paperwork to the other professionals working the deal. She will research and obtain requested documents. She will keep the seller patient during trying times. Buyers are not the only ones to get frustrated. Sellers can become very cantankerous during the time between contract and closing. The broker will maintain harmony between all parties involved.

When the big day comes, the seller's broker will attend the closing. She will be there to answer questions and to handle any last-minute disputes. The closing process can intimidate inexperienced people. When the buyer or the seller becomes confused or nervous, the broker will step in and clarify the situation. Until the deal is closed, her job is not done. Once the closing is complete, the broker will receive her commission and congratulate both parties, laughing all the way to the bank.

This is the way an experienced broker operates. If you are associated with an inexperienced broker, many of these duties may be skipped. They either don't have the experience to know the importance of their role, or feel that one task or another is not their job. Some brokers believe they have earned their commission when the contract is signed and delivered. These brokers soon learn they don't get paid unless the deal closes. Some of the chores may not be in their job description, but if they want steady commission checks, they soon learn to assume responsibility, fast.

THE BUYER'S BROKER

The main difference between a seller's broker and a buyer's broker is the person for whom they work. Both brokers may work with the seller and the purchaser, but only one person pays the broker's fee. This is the determining factor in the role of the broker. A buyer's broker is paid by the purchaser, not the seller. This concept is relatively new, but it has received a warm welcome from informed purchasers. If you examine the situation, retaining a buyer's broker makes a lot of sense.

When you buy your home, will you use the seller's attorney to represent you? Most people insist on having their own attorney instead of using the seller's. This is done to remove any fear that one attorney cannot equally serve two clients in the same deal. There may be no justification in this fear, but it exists. The same principle can be used to compare real estate brokers. The arrangement is not the same, but the mental association applies.

When you deal directly with the seller's broker, you are putting all your trust in someone being paid by the seller. When you allow the seller's attorney to represent you, you are paying the attorney. The fact that you are both paying the same attorney means the attorney has an equal obligation to both of you. This is not true in the case of working directly with

a seller's broker. While the seller's broker must treat you fairly, she has a greater obligation to the seller than to you.

For years, people have dealt with seller's brokers. For the most part, buyers rarely considered the lopsided relationship. To this day, many people believe the listing broker is working for them. This is not true. The listing broker is working *with* the purchaser, but *for* the seller. This distinction is significant. As the public has become better informed, the number of buyer's brokers has increased.

Buyer's brokers perform many of the same duties that the seller's broker does. The big difference is, they work to get *you*, not the seller, the best deal possible. Since the buyer's broker is working for you, you must make an agreement for services to be rendered and payment for these services. This is usually done with a contractual agreement between the purchaser and the buyer's broker.

By hiring a buyer's broker, you know what to expect from the broker. Many buyers will not retain a buyer's broker because of the cost involved. The buyer's broker's fee is negotiated between you and the broker. The fee can be any amount the two of you agree on. Whatever the fee is, you will have to pay it.

In traditional real estate deals, the seller pays the broker's fee. This fee is paid from the proceeds of the sale. In effect, the buyer has always paid the fee, but through the seller. If the seller does not have to pay a commission, he can afford to sell his property for a lower price. If you are paying a higher price because the seller is paying a commission to the broker, you are, in effect, paying the commission indirectly.

The concept of buyer's brokers has gained popularity but has yet to meet with widespread public acceptance. There are many benefits to the buyer when a buyer's broker is retained. You will have to evaluate the cost and the benefits to see if you want to hire a buyer's broker. If you do retain a buyer's broker, he can perform many vital assignments for you.

Your broker can provide you with current market data. This will be helpful in making your buying decision. The broker can consult with you on negotiating strategies. This is something you cannot get from the seller's broker. The buyer's broker can assist you in understanding and obtaining financing. Your broker will work with you to write a purchase offer favoring your position. This is another service you cannot obtain from the seller's broker. The broker can act as your representative in executing inspections and providing information for your removal of contingencies.

A good buyer's broker will provide assistance with all your questions. He will be unbiased in which house you buy. Since you are paying the broker, he will not care which house is sold. This is a big difference between buyer's brokers and seller's brokers. The seller's broker wants you to buy the seller's home. The buyer's broker wants you to buy the home best suited for you.

WHO IS THE BROKER WORKING FOR?

Now that you have an overview of the different types of brokers, let's take a closer look at each of them. If the broker is being paid by the seller, you will want to guard your feelings and reactions. Anything you say about a prospective property will be directly relayed to the seller from most brokers. Unless you insist on creating a buyer's broker agreement, the broker is working for the seller. There will be more on this later in the chapter.

As a prospective home buyer, you may benefit from the assistance of a broker. If you want the broker to work for you, you must enter into a buyer's broker agreement. When you do this, the broker is your agent and will be working with your best interests in mind. The broker will not divulge information received from you without your authorization. These points of the agreement are important in your negotiating power.

As a buyer's broker, the real estate agent will be paid by you. This type of arrangement is relatively new to the real estate industry. For years, real estate brokers were *always* paid by the seller and *always*

worked for the seller. As times change, so do business procedures. As the public has become more informed, it has recognized a need for brokers to work for the buyer. If you are wondering what was wrong with the broker working for the seller and with the buyer, let me explain.

WHO PAYS THE BROKER?

When a broker is being paid by the seller, his first loyalty is to the seller. He must treat buyers fairly and relay accurate information, but he is always working for the seller. This may be difficult to understand when you look at what a seller's broker does for the buyer. As a seller's broker, the agent will perform many duties to help the buyer. The broker may help qualify the buyer for financing. She could work with the buyer to arrange financing through a lender. The broker will meet with the buyer and discuss aspects of the property being considered. The seller's agent will often assist the purchaser in making an offer to purchase the property.

When the seller's agent does so much to help the buyer, it might appear the agent is working for the buyer. She is not. If she is being paid by the seller, she is a seller's broker. What are the drawbacks to you when working with a seller's broker? The largest liability is the broker's allegiance to the seller. While the seller's broker is not obligated to tell you everything the seller says, she is required to relay all your comments to the seller. Due to the many duties performed by the seller's agent for the buyer, it is easy for a relationship to form.

The buyer may come to trust the agent and to rely on her for advice. To some extent, this is okay, but the results can hurt you in negotiations. After many meetings, you may become friendly with the seller's broker. Many buyers believe the seller's broker is working for them and open themselves up to the broker. This is where problems can arise. By law, the broker must relay her dealings with you to the seller. In the bargaining stages, you can lose your edge in negotiations.

EXAMPLE OF WORKING WITH A SELLER'S BROKER

Imagine this scene as an example of how your bargaining strength is lost. You have worked with the seller's broker for several weeks and have come to trust her. You have decided you want to make an offer to purchase the home she has been working with you on. The asking price for the house is $112,700. You call and arrange a meeting with the broker. When you get together, you inform her of your interest in purchasing the house. She says fine and offers to write the offer for you, as per your instructions. She asks how you would like the offer worded.

Since this is your first home, you are not sure what to do. You ask the broker for advice on what she thinks the seller will take for the property. By law, she is only allowed to tell you what the listed sale price of the home is. If she knows the seller will accept a lower amount, she is not allowed to tell you. Remember, she is working for the seller. In answer to your question, the broker agrees to write the offer for any amount you instruct her to. This is a situation where *you* have to make the decision.

You tell the broker you want to offer the seller $107,000 for the house. She then asks you to tell her how to word the written offer. Again, you don't know what should be said, so you ask for her advice. Being the seller's agent, she only gives generic recommendations. Basically, she tells you what has to be in the offer, not what could be in the offer. She asks how you plan to pay for the property and when you want to close on the home. You request a closing date to be set for sixty days from acceptance of the offer.

For financing, it is stipulated that you will apply for a thirty-year, fixed-rate mortgage with an interest rate not to exceed 10.5%. You further detail your plans to provide a 10% down payment for the loan and if the loan is not approved, you may void the contract, without penalty. The broker then asks what you will be giving as an earnest money deposit. When you ask how much you should give, the broker recommends 10% of the offered price. She explains how this will show good faith and financial strength. Not knowing any different, you agree to the 10% deposit.

The broker may ask if you require that any other contingencies be placed in the offer. As a new buyer, you are not aware of all the possible clauses to include. You decide to request a professional inspection of the property. The broker asks how you want the inspection clause worded. You don't know, but you explain you want the inspection to protect you from structural problems with the house. The broker places the contingency in the offer to protect you from structural problems. This type of question-and-answer routine goes along until the offer is completed and signed.

Later that evening, the broker calls you to let you know your offer was accepted by the seller. She brings a copy of the signed contract to you and hand delivers it. When the contract is delivered, it becomes a binding contract. Doing business this way, you were able to place the home you wanted under contract, but there are many potential problems. Study the next example to see how the procedure might have been done differently if you had worked with a buyer's broker.

EXAMPLE OF WORKING WITH A BUYER'S BROKER

After verifying credentials, you have retained a real estate broker to work for you. A buyer's broker agreement has been established; the broker is committed to working for you. After telling the broker the type of house you want, he begins to search for your new home.

The day comes when you have decided to make an offer on a house the broker found for you. The asking price for the house is $112,700. You call and arrange a meeting with your broker. At the meeting, you talk with your agent about the house and the offer. Since you are not sure how to proceed, you ask your broker for advice. In the capacity of a buyer's broker, your agent can offer advice and help with designing the offer. In the first example, the broker agreed to write the offer as you instructed her to. In this example, your broker can guide you in making the offer.

In the first example, you asked the broker for advice on what she thought the seller would accept for the property. By law, she was only allowed to tell you what the listed sale price of the home was. When this same question is posed to your buyer's broker, the results are different. If he feels the seller will accept an amount less than the listed price, he may make known his opinion. The seller's broker, in the first example, was unable to do this. The difference is, your broker is working for you, not the seller. He can give professional advice on market conditions and any information he may know about the seller's motivation to sell.

This is a big advantage for you. If your broker checks for recent comparable sales, he may determine the property is only worth $100,000. This type of verifiable evidence can be used to convince the seller to accept a lower price. If the first broker had shown you this information, she would have been damaging her seller's position. Seller's brokers must try to obtain the listed price for their client's property. Your buyer's broker is obligated to help you make the best deal possible. This one factor can be well worth the expense of a buyer's broker.

In the first example, you did not directly pay the broker for her services. She was paid by the seller, but you paid more for the house. By using a buyer's broker, you are able to prove the house has a market value of $100,000. The $7,000 you save on the price of the house will more than pay for the services of your buyer's broker. This is only one advantage to engaging a broker to work directly for you.

In the earlier example, the broker agreed to write the offer according to terms you described. She was not much help in deciding what should go into the offer. Your buyer's broker can prove invaluable with this stage of the deal. Your broker can explain how the offer might be worded and what different phrases mean to the offer. He might suggest you make a $500 deposit, instead of a full 10% deposit. If the seller requires a larger deposit, he will indicate that in a counter offer.

The smaller deposit keeps most of your money in your bank account. It is not losing interest for you by being in an escrow account somewhere. If something goes wrong, your big money will not be tied up during confrontations. Many offers are written with deposits of only $100. Unless the seller insists on a large deposit, there is no need for one.

When the seller's broker wrote your financing contingency, she wrote it verbatim. The clause could have been written to favor your position more clearly. In the first example, you stipulated applying for a thirty-year, fixed-rate mortgage with an interest rate not to exceed 10.5%. You also stated your plans to provide a 10% down payment for the loan and if the loan was not approved, you reserved the right to void the contract, without penalty. This isn't a bad clause, but it could be better.

There is no mention of discount points in the financing clause. Each discount point is equal to 1% of the loan amount and they can add up quickly. Points are used to lower the interest rate on which payments will be based. If the going rate of interest is 12%, you might get a 10.5% loan rate by paying discount points. In your first clause, there was no limit on the points, and it was assumed you would pay them. If you were not willing to pay points to achieve the 10.5% loan, the seller may have been able to sue you for breach of contract. In doing so, the seller might have had reason to claim your 10% deposit for damages. Paying several points or losing your deposit would be a very expensive way to gain experience.

Since your broker is working for you, he would recommend some common clauses to include in your offer. In the financing clause, he might have added wording to address the payment of points. You could have said you will pay up to, but not more than, two discount points. You could have asked the seller to pay up to, but not more than, two points. By doing this, at the worst you limit your out-of-pocket expenses to two points. At best, the seller agrees to pay the points for you.

In the first example, you included a contingency clause for a professional inspection. The seller's agent wrote the clause exactly as you had stated it. Your buyer's broker would have suggested different wording. The seller's agent didn't suggest additional wording, due to her relationship with the seller. A seller's broker must include all your requests in the offer, but she is not required to advise you of ways to protect yourself. She is working for the seller and wants the contract to be free of all contingencies, whenever possible.

Your original inspection clause partially protected you from structural damage. The clause did not clearly state what your options would be if structural problems were discovered. It should have given you the right to void the contract, without penalty, if structural problems were found. In addition, the clause only pertained to structural problems. It did not cover any of the other numerous problems that could adversely affect the value of the house. These additional problems could have been malfunctioning plumbing, heating, cooling, and electrical systems. You may have found the appliances to be defective. The home could have any number of serious problems beyond structural deficiencies. Any of these defects would not be covered by the original contingency clause.

WORDING IS EVERYTHING

In an offer to purchase real estate, wording is everything. By adding a few simple words, you can be placed under extreme pressure to close on a specific date. Most contracts allow the contract to remain in force if the scheduled closing date passes, but by adding five words to the offer, it changes completely. Adding a phrase after the closing date that states, "time is of the essence," requires the transaction to be closed on or before the scheduled closing date. If it is not, you could be in default and might lose your deposit. By hiring a broker to work directly for you, much of this type of information will be explained to you before the offer to purchase is made. By this example, you should have an idea of what benefits a buyer's broker can be to you.

QUALITIES TO LOOK FOR IN A REAL ESTATE BROKER

Choosing a broker should be done with thought and attention to detail. Finding the right broker can be more difficult than locating the right house. It is important not to get involved with the wrong bro-

ker. Unless you are well-versed in the ways of real estate, many of your decisions will be based on information supplied by your broker. Making the wrong decision on which broker to work with may result in your making poor decisions on which house to buy and how to buy it.

A common reflex is to work with a broker you know. It might be your neighbor or your aerobics teacher. Many real estate brokers have full-time jobs and broker real estate part-time. Just because someone has a license to broker real estate does not mean he is well-suited to be your broker. As a first-time buyer, you may need an experienced professional to guide you through the maze to home ownership. An inexperienced broker could do more harm than good.

Beware of Working with Friends

If you do have friends who are brokers, think twice before working with them. Real estate deals can go bad and when they do, friends may be caught in the middle. It is a good idea to keep your home-buying experience strictly on a business level. Part-time brokers can make good buyer's brokers. The fact that they work part-time is no reason to disqualify them. If they know their business and are attentive to your needs, they will do fine.

Investigate Credentials

Word-of-mouth referrals are among the best ways to find a good broker. Ask your friends and co-workers if they recommend anyone. If they do, ask how they know about the broker's professional ability. If they purchased property through the broker, it is probably a good reference. If the broker is their brother-in-law or their tennis partner, the reference may lose some of its credibility. In either case, do your own investigation of brokers you are considering.

When you interview potential brokers, ask for a list of at least five recent references. These should be people the broker worked with in the last six months. Call the local licensing agency to see if the broker has ever been found at fault from a consumer complaint. After a thorough investigation, make your decision based on facts. If you want a broker to work directly for you, verify that the broker has experience as a buyer's broker. Being a buyer's broker is significantly different from being a seller's broker. If the broker is inexperienced, he probably is not going to earn the money you pay him.

A good buyer's broker should have most, if not all, of the following credentials:

- Evidence of continuing education in the real estate business.
- A current real estate license, in good standing.
- A comprehensive knowledge of market conditions.
- The ability to communicate well with others.
- Membership in a multiple listing service.
- A list of recently satisfied clients.
- An established business reputation.
- A strong knowledge of financing.
- Experience as a buyer's broker.

DO YOU NEED A BROKER?

As a buyer, you may not need a buyer's broker. You can learn a great deal about real estate from reading. Seller's brokers will be anxious to work with you and to show you what is available for sale in the real estate market. If you retain a good real estate attorney, develop a background of basic real estate knowledge, and don't sign anything without your attorney's approval, you can get by without a buyer's broker.

The key to having an enjoyable experience from purchasing your first home is *knowledge*. Whether you learn the knowledge from reading or obtain it from a broker doesn't matter. The broker offers the advantage of knowing the local and current real estate market. He can make your house-buying procedure go more smoothly and quickly. Books can teach you the basics, but they cannot account for each market and ever-changing market conditions. Your attorney will know real estate law, but he may not be in touch with current market conditions.

The simple answer to the question of whether you need a broker is "no." You do not *need* one, but he can make your life much easier. Without a broker, you will have to depend on yourself for making field decisions. An attorney can only do so much; the rest is up to you. Seller's brokers will provide some of the information you need, but not enough. Buyer's broker rates vary, but the brokers earn their money. If they do the job the way it should be done, they earn every penny.

COMMON DUTIES OF A BUYER'S BROKER

- Qualify the purchaser for financing and determine the maximum loan amount the buyer may obtain.
- Educate the buyer on available financing.
- Assist the buyer in defining housing needs.
- Provide the buyer with current market condition information.
- Seek out potential homes for the purchaser.
- Participate in the showing of homes under consideration.
- Consult with the buyer to answer any real estate questions.
- Advise the buyer on procedures he may wish to follow.
- Assist the buyer in establishing a fair market value for a home.
- Assist the buyer in drafting a purchase offer.
- Deliver the purchase offer.
- Mediate offer negotiations.
- Assist the buyer in obtaining financing.
- Provide follow-up service on all aspects of the transaction.
- Attend the closing with buyer.

If you stop to think about it, a competent broker performs a lot of important tasks *for you*. After completing this book, you should have a good idea of whether you will need a buyer's broker.

BUYER'S BROKER DISADVANTAGES

There are very few disadvantages to working with a good broker. One reasonable disadvantage to consider is the reluctance of some sellers to work with brokers. If you are looking for homes being sold directly by the owner, a broker may not be well received. Some sellers resent paying brokers and refuse to work with them. Even if you are paying the broker, the seller may not be willing to cooperate. This disadvantage runs parallel to one of the advantages.

When sellers refuse to talk to your buyer's broker, they may be hiding something. Professional brokers know how to discover items the average home buyer would never notice. Something like a water line on the basement wall could tip the broker to a house with a leaky basement. If the basement is dry when you look at it, you might not notice the water line. The buyer is emotionally involved, and excitement overtakes logic at times. A good broker throttles this natural exuberance and counter-balances the effect with his professional approach.

The only other disadvantage is money. Buyer's brokers charge a fee for their services. If you feel qualified to act in your own behalf, this fee could be a disadvantage. More times than not, a good broker earns the fee. If he keeps you from making a mistake in the purchase, you may have saved thousands of dollars by retaining the broker.

The advantages of working with a buyer's broker are numerous. Refer to the list of duties the broker commonly performs. Are you prepared to complete all those duties? First-time buyers are vulnerable to mistakes. Anytime you are doing something for the first time, you are more likely to make a mistake. Evaluate your personal abilities and determine whether you are capable of working without a buyer's broker. Beware of working too closely with seller's brokers and insist on having all documents reviewed by your attorney before signing them.

THERE IS NO TURNING BACK

Following this advice will put you well down the road to home ownership. Without considering these facts, your first purchase could result in disaster. Real estate transactions are serious business. In most cases, once you sign on the dotted line, there is no turning back. If you approach home buying with respect, you will become a happy homeowner. Looking at the deal as a real-life game can ruin your future plans. Before you run blindly into the world of real estate, get to know the rules. Buying your first home is much more complicated than it was in your parents' time. Laws and rules change each year. It is important for you to act on current information.

6

What to Look for in Your First Home

Buying a home is a big decision. It requires much more than simply seeing a house you like and buying it. Of course, one of the initial steps in deciding on a home is its appearance. If you don't like a home's style or physical characteristics, the consideration process ends and your search continues. This part of the decision-making process is easy. If you don't like the house, you don't buy it. Once you do find a property you like, the evaluation procedure becomes more complicated.

THE FIRST WALK-THROUGH INSPECTION

During your first visit to the home, keep in mind the needs and desires you established in Chapter 2. Once a property conforms to your criteria, visually gather essential information to make an intelligent decision. Always bring paper and pencils with you when viewing properties. A small tape recorder makes a handy addition to a pad and pencil. As you walk through the home, draw a rough sketch of the layout and various room sizes. Often, the broker or seller will have actual room dimensions on a listing sheet. This data will help you determine later if the house will meet your needs and accommodate your furniture. After you tour the house, go outside and look at the lot and the exterior. By this time, your emotions may be taking control of you. That's all right. The first walk-through is meant to give you an overall feel for the property.

REMAIN TIGHT-LIPPED

When a home passes the test of an initial walk-through inspection, it is time to start giving serious thought to the purchase. If you are working with a broker, thank her for showing the home and tell her you will get back to her with your decision. She will probably push you for some type of comment on the house. Avoid giving the broker any reaction to the property. Even brokers who appear to be working with you are usually working for and are paid by the home's seller. Any comments or reaction you give will be directly conveyed to the seller. Your negotiating position can be weakened when your first impressions are disclosed to the brokers and seller.

PUT YOUR FEELINGS ON PAPER

If you are serious about the property, don't look at any others that day. When you view too many houses, it is easy to confuse one home's features with another's. Go home or to a quiet, private place, and evaluate your impression of the property. Take a sheet of paper and record your feelings about the home. List your likes and dislikes. This list will assist you in remembering various aspects of the home. Begin this procedure as soon after seeing the home as possible. Your memory will be fresh, and your thoughts will flow smoothly.

Once you have noted all the aspects of the home you can remember, review the list. Note all facets of the property you don't clearly recall. In addition to the categories on your list, compile any questions you may have. This exercise will generate an inspection sheet for the second showing of the home.

SET UP A SECOND SHOWING

When you have included every item you can't remember or have questions about, call your broker. Schedule a time to see the home again. If you initially looked at the home during the day, try to schedule the second showing at night. House features can appear dramatically different under various conditions. At night, incandescent lighting can expose flaws in areas such as walls and ceilings — cracks you never noticed before. Ask the broker to request that the sellers be present for this showing. Plan on spending at least an hour doing the walk-through and asking questions. If the seller is unwilling or unable to attend the showing, you should still go for the second tour.

Take a notebook and your checklists with you for this second showing. Perform a methodical inspection of the home until all the blanks on the checklists contain comments. During the inspection, list in the notebook any questions you have. Prepare these questions during the inspection; don't wait until you have completed the tour to list them. Writing down your questions as you go will reduce the likelihood of forgetting or omitting something. This second inspection is crucial in your decision-making process; gathering thorough information is an essential part of the inspection.

GETTING A REALISTIC LOOK

You will notice things on this inspection that were overlooked on the initial walk-through. The purpose of the first showing was to establish an interest in the home. This follow-up inspection is designed to bypass your emotions and provide a realistic look at the quality of the property. When you are satisfied that you have examined all aspects of the home, try to have your questions answered directly by the seller. You will benefit from seeing and hearing the owner's reaction to your questions. Sometimes, you can learn more from facial expressions and voice inflections than you can from the answer itself.

THE INTERROGATION PROCESS

The listing broker should have provided you with an information and disclosure sheet at your first showing. Review these documents at this time and confirm the accuracy of the information with the seller. Then proceed with the list of questions you have developed from the two showings. If the seller is not present, ask your broker to make a photocopy of your list and to present the questions to the seller.

PROFESSIONAL HOME INSPECTIONS

When all your questions have been answered, you can continue with the next phase of the selection process. Assuming you are still interested in the home, you will need to arrange for a professional home inspection. These inspections are typically priced between $125 and $300. It is best for you to come to terms on a price for the house before scheduling the inspection. You may wish to present an offer to purchase the house with a contingency clause.

MAKING YOUR FIRST OFFER

Under these conditions, your offer would be subject to receiving a satisfactory professional home inspection report. Depending on the results of this inspection, you would have various options. If the report exposes costly problems, you would be allowed to withdraw your offer and have your earnest-money deposit returned. At that point, all you have invested is the cost of the inspection. This has proven to be money well spent. Another option would be to offer a lower price, as a form of compensation for the home's deficiencies and the inevitable repair costs you will incur.

This approach is common and should be acceptable to the seller. By using this method, you are not spending your money on an inspection needlessly. However, if you have the inspection done prior to a contingency offer, there is no guarantee the seller will accept your offer. Once an offer is in the works, the seller is much more likely to be open to negotiations on the home. It is even possible for you to recover your inspection cost by bargaining for a lower sale price. These techniques are discussed in further detail in Chapters 10 and 12.

WHAT TO LOOK FOR

Now that you know the chronological order of inspecting a home, let's discuss what you should look for. The features affecting a home's value are many. For the average individual, it is very difficult to think of all the items to scrutinize. Professional inspections are needed for the technical components of the house, but they don't deal with the personal aspect of your decision. You must assume full responsibility for determining whether the property is suitable to you. Without an outline to follow, many of these vital characteristics will be overshadowed with excitement. If you eliminate as many potential problems as possible now, you will have plenty of time to be elated after you own the home.

The remainder of this chapter lists primary elements to consider about your intended purchase. These factors should all be accounted for and classified. The time you spend completing a thorough inspection will protect your financial investment. It can save you money on repairs and will ensure your satisfaction with the home.

LOCATION

Location is one of the most important influencing factors in the value of real estate. Does the location of this house meet your needs? Will it also meet the needs of the buying public when you are ready to sell? Are there good schools in the area? Is shopping convenient? Are transportation routes suitable for commuting workers? Consider what the driving conditions will be like under bad weather conditions. Are there low bridges that might flood, steep hills to cope with in the snow, or difficult intersections to navigate? Are there any underlying deterrents to the location of the property? Examples might include landfills, nuclear power stations, industrial sites, or other equally undesirable neighbors.

REAL ESTATE TAXES

Confirm the current annual taxes for the property. This information should be provided on the property data sheet supplied by the listing broker. There is no reason you cannot obtain tax figures. Ask the seller to confirm the figure and check with the local tax assessor to verify the tax amount. This information is a matter of public record and easily accessible. Exorbitant taxes can destroy the affordability of a property.

LIENS

Request detailed information on any outstanding mortgages, liens, or judgments against the property. Ask for a statement guaranteeing there is no risk of upcoming mechanic's liens or materialman's liens. Often, sellers will have improvements made before putting a house on the market. If work goes unpaid, liens could result. These encumbrances could be placed on the house, even after the transfer of ownership to you. This is an often overlooked but vitally important aspect of deciding whether a home is suitable for purchase.

TYPES OF UTILITIES AND SERVICES

In addition to the electrical service, what other public services and utilities are available? Find out if natural gas is used in the operation of the home's equipment. Are any of the house's systems operated by oil? If oil is used, ascertain where the oil storage tank is located. Does the storage tank comply with local requirements? Underground oil tanks can create a costly problem for new home buyers. If these tanks must be removed to comply with environmental protection rules or local codes, the cost can be staggering.

Many times, properties are protected under grandfathered regulations or special variances. When the property is sold, these special permissions may not extend to the purchaser. As the new owner, you may be responsible for the mandatory removal of the storage tank. Check this possibility thoroughly before committing to a property. Find out if the home's plumbing is connected to public water and sewer facilities. What are the fees for these services? Is the house located on a public or private road? People who use private streets are often required to pay fees to maintain the road and for snow removal. Will your home's garbage be collected by the municipality, or will you be required to make arrangements for private disposal? Is cable television available?

UTILITY COSTS

Document the historical cost of all utilities provided to the home. It should be easy for the seller or utility companies to provide you with actual heating and electrical cost figures. Annual operation costs may make one house more desirable than another.

COVENANTS AND RESTRICTIONS

Request a copy of all covenants and restrictions and ask for the zoning status of the property. First-time buyers often consider a property based on its expansion potential. You might think the house will be perfect after building the garage of your dreams. Your dream can be shattered by the influence of covenants, restrictions, and zoning ordinances. You may be distressed to find that you don't have enough land to allow the construction of a garage.

Most areas require certain setbacks from property lines for any construction. This means you probably will not be able to build on all the land surrounding the house. Covenants and restrictions are placed on areas by the developers. Their purpose is to maintain a quality of housing in the neighborhood. The intent is noble, but these restrictions may prohibit you from making the changes you desire. This information can be obtained from the Registry of Deeds and the Zoning Board office.

If the property is located in a planned community, many regulations may affect the changes you can make. I know of one such neighborhood that prohibits homeowners from painting their houses a different color, changing a mailbox, or adding an exterior light, without prior approval from the board of directors. You can see why it is important to investigate all restrictions applying to the home you are considering.

ASSOCIATION FEES AND SERVICES

Many newer subdivisions provide amenities for the neighborhood residents. When you assess the home's location, you may be impressed with these recreational provisions. Common facilities include swimming pools, tennis courts, health and fitness cen-

ters, and numerous others. Don't assume that you have access to these services without cost.

In planned developments, there are frequently association fees required of all homeowners. The fees vary in amount and are used to maintain the facilities. If you are not aware of these additional expenses, you may wind up in financial trouble. The monthly association fee, combined with your house payment, may put a house beyond your reach.

DISASTER INSURANCE REQUIREMENTS

Some homes that appear perfectly normal may be difficult and expensive to insure. Houses located in flood plains and flood zones are extreme examples. Flood insurance may be complicated to obtain, and it will always be expensive. The lender providing your mortgage funding will require insurance to protect a security interest. Inquire about any unusual insurance that may be required due to the location or condition of the home.

PROPOSED CHANGES IN THE SURROUNDINGS

Long-range development plans can have a negative impact on a property's value. Ask the seller, the broker, and the local planning commission about any anticipated future changes for the area. The construction of roads, industrial parks, or low-cost housing projects may disqualify the house from your consideration.

THE LAWN

In warm weather, look for consistency in grass cover. Does the soil support a healthy lawn and resist erosion? Are there any dead or dying trees to be removed? Is the lot properly graded to allow adequate drainage? Ask the seller if there are any areas of the lawn that are soggy or collect water. Are there any ground depressions from old stumps that will have to be filled in? Do you notice any unusual odors from the air or ground? If the house has a sump pump, where does the pump's discharge go?

Many houses with water problems depend on sump pumps to keep their foundation area dry. If the discharge from these pumps is dumped into the yard, it will erode the soil and cause lawn care problems. Rain gutters are another common source of difficulty. Are the gutter downspouts piped into a drainage system, or do they dump into the lawn?

GARAGES AND OUTBUILDINGS

Rate the overall appearance of these buildings. Do they enhance or detract from the home's curb appeal? Are the structures in keeping with the architectural design of the neighborhood? In regards to the physical condition of these buildings, follow the same steps used in evaluating the home. One thing to pay special attention to is the foundations and possible termite damage of these buildings.

These after-thought structures may not have been constructed by qualified professionals. The foundations may not be adequate and could cause structural problems. Since these buildings are not a part of the house, they may not have been protected from termite infestation. When you request professional home inspection, request a detailed report on these detached buildings as well.

WELLS AND SEPTIC SYSTEMS

Locate the well and septic system before making your offer to purchase. What is the depth and recovery rate of the well? Are there times of the year when water conservation is mandatory to maintain your well's water level? Has a current water test been made? You should request water test results before making your final decision to buy. Many people are sensitive to mineral and acid levels in well water. Look at the toilets to see if the water has discolored the china. This is a good indication of high mineral levels in the water. Ask the seller to tell you how far the well is from the septic system. Ideally, there should be at least 100 feet between the water you drink and the waste-disposal system for your house.

Ask when the septic tank was last pumped out. You should also find out what type of material the septic tank is made of. If it is an old metal tank, you may have to replace it. Is the drain field the proper size for the present size of the home? When homes are expanded or remodeled, the septic system is rarely upgraded. This could present problems with the effectiveness of the septic disposal system. It will also be an indication of the feasibility of any expansion plans you may have for the property. Ask the sellers if they have had problems with the system in the past.

EXTERIOR CONSTRUCTION

Style: Is the home built to similar standards of surrounding houses? Are the style and method of construction compatible with the neighborhood?

Foundation: Inspect the overall appearance and check for cracks or loose bricks. Are the mortar joints level? If they are not, the house may have a sinking foundation. Are the mortar joints firm, or are they sandy and easily removed? If the joints are sandy, the foundation work will need masonry attention to maintain its integrity.

Siding: Is the siding flat and level? If the siding is rippled or buckling, you may have found a bad foundation or moisture problem. To detect curves in the siding, stand at the corners of the house and look along each exterior wall.

Paint: Is the paint in good condition, or is it fading? Consider how long it will be before you have to repaint the exterior. If the paint is cracking or peeling, the house may have a serious moisture problem.

Doors: Do the exterior doors seal well? Are they easy to open or do they stick? Sticking doors may be the result of poor installation, swelling, or a sagging foundation. How is the wood around the doors? Is it firm and well-painted or soft and spongy? If it is spongy, rot has invaded the wood and the wood trim will require replacement.

Windows: Windows should be inspected like the doors. Check the same components to establish the condition of the windows. Very few people remember to open every window in the house. Bedroom windows are particularly important as a form of emergency exit. I once inspected a house where the windows were screwed shut. Upon removing the screws, I found several windows fell right out of their frames. Check the glazing to make sure the glass is solidly installed in the window frame.

If the home has a bay window, look for metal flashing where the window's roof meets the siding. If this connection is not flashed, you should expect water leakage into the home's exterior wall or the ceiling of the window. The weatherstripping in older windows will often bind the operation of the unit. Broken springs have the opposite effect; they prevent the window from staying open.

Roof: Step back and inspect the roof from the front, back, and sides. If the roof sags, it could be a bad roof structure or a bad foundation. Are the shingles in good repair or are they cracked and turned up? If the roof looks brittle or inconsistent, you will probably have leaks in the near future.

Chimneys: If the chimney is installed along the exterior of the home, check for a foundation and flashing. Without a solid foundation, the chimney could pull away from the house as it settles into the ground. If there is no flashing where the chimney meets the siding, water may leak into the walls.

Decks and porches: Do the decks and porches have sufficient foundations? When you walk on decks and porches, they should not shake or bounce. Study the area where the deck or porch connects to the house. Discoloration reveals areas of siding unaffected by weather and may indicate the deck is sinking or pulling away from the house. Is the deck made with pressure-treated lumber to withstand the outside elements? Are the handrails and steps sturdy? Don't forget to inspect porch roofs and screening as well.

INTERIOR CONSTRUCTION

Foundation: If the house is built on a crawlspace foundation, check for water problems, proper ventilation, and a moisture-control ground cover. Crawlspaces should have a plastic vapor barrier on the ground. It should cover 80% of the total ground surface, but not all of the ground. Houses need some moisture; if the ground is completely covered with plastic, dry rot may occur. The foundation vents should be spaced to allow adequate cross-ventilation. Wear work clothes and bring a flashlight to the second showing of the home. You may not like the idea of crawling under the house, but this is better than discovering troublesome problems after you buy it. Standing water, or evidence of it, can cause structural problems and increase mold and mildew growth. It can also cause paint to crack and peel.

Basements: If the house has a basement, look for evidence of water problems. Stained walls and musty odors indicate the presence of water. Are the mechanical systems sitting on the floor or up on blocks or pallets? If they are on the floor, check to see if the bottoms of the heating unit and water heater show indications of rust. Another strong indication of water trouble is if the owner's personal possessions are suspended from the ceiling or piled on blocks. Check for any visible cracks or flaking in the foundation walls or the floor. Look up, and check for mildew stains on the floor joists over your head.

Is there a sump pump in the basement? These pumps are used for one thing only: removing water. Properly installed drain tile and sump pump systems can eliminate the problems caused by a high water table. Water problems may be seasonal or regular. If you plan to use the basement for habitable space or extensive storage, water problems can ruin your plans.

Design: Once you determine that you like the house, examine the floor plan. Analyze the traffic patterns from the kitchen to the exterior door and from the bedrooms to the bathroom. Will you have to carry your groceries through the living room to get to the kitchen? Must you go upstairs to use the bathroom? Will you mind carrying clothes up two flights of stairs from the basement to the bedrooms on the second floor? Look at the basic room layouts.

Will it be difficult to place furniture in a room because of the location of windows and doors? Is there adequate closet space, especially in the bedrooms? Is there a coat closet convenient to the front door and a linen closet near the bathroom? Judge the storage capabilities of the home. A three-bedroom house with only three closets for storage can pose a problem. Some people don't like the open living concept. They do not want their guests watching from the living room while they cook in the kitchen. Others prefer the spacious appearance created by cased openings and unobstructed rooms. Ask yourself if the house feels comfortable.

Floors: Do the floors sag or squeak? As you walk through the house, bounce on the floors to see if articles in the room rattle and shake. These symptoms could indicate a need for additional floor support. Moisture can also cause floors to warp or bulge. If possible, look to see what type of flooring is under the carpet. You may even be pleasantly surprised to find hardwood floors hiding under the carpet. Not all of your examinations will reveal negative features.

Floor coverings: Are the wood floors in good condition or are they stained black from moisture? Does the carpet bounce back from your footsteps or do you leave a path when you walk across the floor? A good carpet pad will spring back; a worn one will not. Is the vinyl floor bubbled, wrinkled, or torn? The seams in vinyl products should not be easily visible. Study the edges where vinyl flooring meets the base molding. Is the vinyl curling up at all?

Interior doors: Do the doors operate smoothly? Some common problems to be aware of are: loose hinges, scraping across the carpet, loose door handles, handles that won't lock, doors that won't stay closed, and doors that stick. If you are right-handed, a good way to test doors is to open them with your left hand. Using your weaker hand is a strong demonstration of how easily the door operates.

Walls: Are the walls straight or bowed? Out-of-plumb walls can indicate structural problems. Are the wall coverings in good condition? Look at the number of items the seller has hung from the walls. Does a teenager have a myriad of posters pinned to the walls? Will you have to patch dozens of holes when you move in? Examine the general condition and appearance of the paint.

Ceilings: Are the ceilings flat or do they dip and sag? If ceilings are not level, you could again be faced with structural problems. Are there any spots or stains to indicate water damage? Do you see any changes in paint color or texture? This telltale sign can expose previous problems from water leaks.

Lighting: Do all the rooms have adequate lights? Do they all work properly? Turn on all the lights in the bathrooms and look in the mirrors. Once you own the home, you may be doing this over 2,000 times a year, so make sure the lighting is acceptable. Make a note of whether there are ceiling lights in the bedrooms or lamps. This arrangement is strictly personal preference, but many buyers like ceiling lights in the bedrooms.

Insulation: What is the type and amount of insulation in the walls, floors, and attic? Insulation efficiency is gauged by the product's resistance to heat flow, or R-value. The higher the R-value, the better the insulation's ability to prevent heat loss. Often, insulation will be described in terms of inches. With fiberglass batt (rolled) insulation, R-11 is 3 ½ inches thick and R-19 is 6 inches thick. The resistance value of cellulose blown-in products, about 6 inches thick, is approximately R-19. Houses built prior to the mid-'50s were limited to attic insulation, if any. Try to determine the age of the insulation, because time deteriorates the insulating quality of some older products.

Attic: Is there ventilation for the attic? Does the roof sheathing show any signs of water damage? Do the rafters and ceiling joists appear strong and in good condition? These structural members should not be twisted or bowed. Can you see daylight through any areas of the attic? Examine the attic for feasible storage or expansion benefits.

APPLIANCES

Is the house equipped with the appliances you desire? If you are supplying appliances, will they fit and operate in the spaces available for them? Turn on the stove; run the garbage disposal and dishwasher. Confirm that the existing appliances function properly. Find out exactly which appliances are included in the sales price. Is there an outside vent for your clothes dryer? Is the range hood vented to the outside? Inspect the operation and condition of all appliances conveying with the sale.

PEST CONTROL

Has the house been treated to prevent insect infestation? Is there any pre-existing damage from termites, ants, powder-post beetles, or borers? As part of your contingency offer, you should arrange for a professional pest-control company to examine the house. These inspections can frequently be obtained without cost. Wood-infesting insects can destroy a home and the cost to remove them can run into thousands of dollars.

AIR CONDITIONING

Does the home have air conditioning? Is it combined with the heating system or is it an independent system? How old is the cooling unit? Is the duct work insulated? What company has the seller used to service the unit? Has the equipment received routine maintenance? If the house has been remodeled or added to, ask your professional inspector to confirm that the existing system is adequate. Even if it is December, test the air conditioning to make sure it works.

HEATING SYSTEM

This first step is to determine what type of heating system the home has. Is it forced hot air, hot-water baseboard, radiators, steam, or electric? Some homes are primarily heated by wood stoves. When approving a mortgage, many lenders will not accept wood as the sole source of heat. Consider also the possible complications of small children around wood stoves. Be sure all levels of the house are heated.

Check each room for a heat source, especially laundry rooms and foyers. In older homes, it is not uncommon for the upstairs to have limited heat vents or none at all for the bedrooms. In the appraisal process, the lack of heated bedrooms can dramatically reduce the value of the home. Most people assume there is heat throughout the house;

don't make this mistake. Verify the outlets for heat in all areas of the habitable space. As with the air conditioning, turn on the heat to make sure it works, regardless of the time of year. Forced hot air and electric systems should dispense heat within a few minutes, while hot water and steam heat may take half an hour.

If the house has been remodeled or expanded, is the existing heating system adequate? What is the age of the heating source? In steam or hot-water systems, how do the supply and return pipes look? Are the fittings leaking or rusting? Will it be difficult to fill the oil tank or work on problems with the system? All aspects of the heating system should be easy to access and operate.

PLUMBING

Are there any obvious leaks in the water distribution or drainage piping? Do all the plumbing fixtures work efficiently? Flush toilets several times. Check to see if the tank continues to run or if the bowl fills slowly. Fill sinks and tubs, then release the water. This will expose slow-running drains. Do the faucets drip? Check for discoloration from dripping water in the tub and sink bowls. Test shower heads, dishwashers, garbage disposers, and ice makers. Examine outside hose-bibbs. These may have frozen in the past and never been repaired.

Check the flooring around the toilet. This is a common place for water leakage and flooring damage. Try to rock the toilet gently to see if it is securely attached to the floor. Run the hot water for at least ten minutes. Does it become hot quickly and stay hot for the entire time? If the water cools during extended use, you will need a new water heater element, mixing-valve, or domestic coil. Locate the source of hot water. Does it come from an electric or gas water heater? Is it provided from a domestic coil integrated into the heating system's boiler? How old is the water heating unit? What is the capacity and recovery rate of the water heater?

If the house receives its water from a well, inspect the interior well equipment. How large is the water storage tank? Is it protected from freezing? Test the tank by running the cold water for several minutes. You can do this to fill the sinks and tubs for their drainage test. If the pump cuts on before the tank is below twenty pounds of pressure, the water storage tank may need to be waterlogged. (When a storage tank is waterlogged, it has too much water and not enough air in it. This causes the well pump to cycle on and off more than it should, wearing out the pump. The tank must be drained, charged with air pressure, and refilled with water.) To test the water pressure, turn on all the faucets and flush the toilet at the same time. Watch for a dramatic decrease in the water flow. Locating the main water shut-off valve during your inspection will prove helpful once you own the home.

ELECTRICAL

Test all electrical appliances, outlets, and lights. Buy an inexpensive night light and bring it with you to test the outlets. You may wish to purchase an inexpensive tester designed to provide detailed information on the wiring. These items are available in most hardware stores for less than $10. When plugged into an outlet, they deliver all the facts you should be concerned with in the wiring to the outlets. Determine whether the house has a fused electrical service or a circuit breaker panel. Is it a 60, 100, or 200 amp service panel? The average home should have at least 100 amp service. If the house has an electric stove and electric heat or is larger than 3,000 square feet, 200 amp service is called for. Check to see if the bathrooms have ground-fault outlets. Are the kitchen counter outlets on a split circuit? If they aren't, you may experience frequent circuit overloads, blown fuses, or tripped breakers. How old is the wiring? Are there adequate outlets in each room to eliminate the need for extension cords (which may be fire hazards)?

OTHER QUESTIONS TO ASK

Does the siding or flooring contain asbestos? Is there any known asbestos in the house? Has the property been subjected to air and water radon tests? Has the potable (drinking) water been tested for bacteria? Has the water been tested for hardness, acidity, iron, or other elements requiring filtration or conditioning? Were the proper permits obtained for all improvements made to the property? Check with the building official's office and the zoning office to see if there are any existing building or zoning code violations.

Don't be intimidated by the number of items to be inspected or your ability to check them. You are about to invest years of hard-earned money into this purchase; you owe it to yourself to get the best property possible for your money. The professional home inspector will evaluate the technical aspects of the home. It is up to you to make sure the house will satisfy your personal needs and desires. This inspection information should be used as a guide. It provides you with enough knowledge to keep brokers and inspectors on their toes.

When you pose these questions, professionals will assume you are knowledgeable about home construction. Inspectors will do a thorough job, and brokers will be less likely to try to slide little items past you. These direct, point-blank inquiries should get a definitive answer. You are buying into a world of potential problems if brokers or sellers can't answer the majority of your questions.

The form in the back of the chapter will serve as your outline for the inspections. If you complete the form, you will have covered the standard elements of a residential inspection. If a swimming pool or other specialty items is included in the sale, consult professionals in those fields. This may seem like a lot of work for you and an inconvenience for the seller, but buying a house is your biggest investment. Without the proper inspections, you are taking a high-stakes gamble. Investing a little time and money now can save you years of frustration and needless expense.

HOME INSPECTION CHECKLIST

ITEM	OK	NOT GOOD	NEED INFO	ITEM	OK	NOT GOOD	NEED INFO
Location	❏	❏	❏	Doors	❏	❏	❏
Taxes	❏	❏	❏	Windows	❏	❏	❏
Liens	❏	❏	❏	Roof	❏	❏	❏
Utilities Available	❏	❏	❏	Chimney	❏	❏	❏
Services	❏	❏	❏	Decks/Porches	❏	❏	❏
Utility Costs	❏	❏	❏	Basement	❏	❏	❏
Covenants	❏	❏	❏	Interior Design	❏	❏	❏
Restrictions	❏	❏	❏	Floors	❏	❏	❏
Association Fees	❏	❏	❏	Floor Coverings	❏	❏	❏
Association Services	❏	❏	❏	Interior Doors	❏	❏	❏
				Walls	❏	❏	❏
Insurance				Ceilings	❏	❏	❏
Requirements	❏	❏	❏	Lighting	❏	❏	❏
Future Development				Insulation	❏	❏	❏
Effects	❏	❏	❏	Attic	❏	❏	❏
Lawn	❏	❏	❏	Appliances	❏	❏	❏
Garage	❏	❏	❏	Structural			
Outbuilding	❏	❏	❏	Condition	❏	❏	❏
Well	❏	❏	❏	Air Conditioning	❏	❏	❏
Septic System	❏	❏	❏	Heating System	❏	❏	❏
Style	❏	❏	❏	Plumbing	❏	❏	❏
Foundation	❏	❏	❏	Electrical	❏	❏	❏
Siding	❏	❏	❏	Hazardous			
Paint	❏	❏	❏	Substances	❏	❏	❏

COMMENTS

7
Finding Hidden Treasure

Many people view buying their first home as a dream. They associate home ownership with prestige and stability. For many, owning a home is an escape from apartment living, annual rent increases, and high income taxes. In the excitement of buying a first home, the value of the financial investment is rarely considered. If a new buyer can own a home, any home, he feels grateful. Yet a first home is definitely a financial investment.

Historically, real estate values appreciate each year. This annual appreciation allows your investment to grow quickly. If you are paying rent, all you have to look forward to next year is higher rent. Since you need a place to live, you might as well make your residence an investment. Buying a home gives you many financial advantages.

Owning a home will reduce your income tax liability, resulting in more money for you. It is not unusual for the first-time home buyer to reduce his or her income tax by $125 or more per month. This tax savings is like having a house payment $125 less than the actual payment. If you were not receiving the tax advantages of home ownership, you would be spending the money on income taxes. Money spent on taxes will not help you build your net worth or retirement fund. Investing in your home will perform both of these functions.

CONTROLLING YOUR MONTHLY HOUSING EXPENSE

When you buy a home, you will know what your monthly payment is. Depending on the loan, you will know what the payments will be each month for as long as you own the home. When renting, you never know how much your rent will increase. As a renter, you are at the mercy of the rental market. Buying a home puts you in control of your monthly housing expense. This allows you to budget your money better and protects you from runaway housing costs.

EQUITY FACTORS

The equity in your home provides peace of mind. If an unexpected emergency arises, you have collateral for a loan. The equity you build in a home can be used to secure a loan. Rent receipts are not worth much when applying for a loan, but equity opens the door to loan approval. Equity can be built in several ways. Each month you make a house payment, you are building equity. In the early years, most of your monthly payment is interest. Very little equity is built from the monthly payments. To build equity fast, you will have to rely on creativity and annual appreciation.

Most of this chapter is designed to show you how to find unusual value in your first home. Before we go on a treasure hunt, let me show you the effect of annual appreciation. For the example, assume you have just purchased a $100,000 home. You made a $5,000 down payment and paid $4,000 in closing costs and points. In the following example, I am going to compare buying this home to making a cash investment. To keep the example simple, I am not going to factor in tax advantages or equity gained through monthly payments. In reality, the results of the example would be better than those shown because of the multiple advantages of home ownership.

EXAMPLE OF ANNUAL APPRECIATION

When you bought your home, you spent $9,000 in cash. This represents your out-of-pocket investment. The remaining value of the home has been financed and is not costing you anything. If you were not making house payments, you would be paying rent and higher income taxes. Annual appreciation rates for real estate vary with the economy and the location of the real estate. Appreciation rates are frequently 5% or more. In very progressive areas, the rate can go to 15% or more. For this example, assume an annual appreciation rate of 7%.

Can you guess what your $100,000 home will be worth in five years? Your $9,000 investment in a $100,000 home will be worth about $141,700 in five years. This means your home has earned an average of more than $8,000 each year. This is a pretty good income for a $9,000 investment. If you had invested the $9,000 in a certificate of deposit (CD), what would you have in five years?

Assume your CD yields an annual interest rate of 10%. A 10% interest rate on a CD is very liberal, as many pay less than 8%. After five years, your $9,000 CD would be worth approximately $14,800. This is nearly $27,000 less than the money you earned with your house. The CD didn't give you a place to live or reduce your income taxes. Which was the better investment? I know that's a stupid question, but I want you to recognize your home as a financial investment.

ON THE TRAIL TO TREASURE

When most people decide to buy a house, they follow the same general path. They talk with real estate brokers and read the advertisements in the paper. For the majority, this is how the public finds a home. Houses advertised in the paper are usually priced at or above their fair-market value. When brokers are involved, the prices may be even higher. If you buy one of these properties, there will be little room in the appraisal for extra equity.

As a smart buyer, you are looking for houses with hidden value or those priced below appraised value.

These properties sometimes show up in the paper, but you must know what to look for. When you see a house advertised with promises of a below-market value, be careful. These obvious deals may be a bad buy. With any acquisition, you must confirm the property's value before making an offer to purchase it. When an ad promises instant equity, double-check the home for a hook. Only in rare cases will you be given something for nothing.

Are you wondering how you will find rewarding properties if they are not advertised? Well, I didn't say they wouldn't be advertised, I said you had to know what to look for. Many of the best buys will not be advertised *where you would expect to find them*. If you enjoy playing detective, finding a home with super value will be fun. When you are not pressed to buy within a certain time, you can almost certainly take advantage of great deals.

Buying your first home will not make you an overnight millionaire, but it could be your first step to financial freedom. Real estate has made more people rich than you can count. Right now, you are looking for your first home. By the time you buy it, you may be addicted to real estate investing. Your trek towards home ownership could be the beginning of a very profitable future. This book is dedicated to helping you buy your first home, but the methods can be applied to other properties. If you enjoy the search for and discovery of your first home, you may be a natural real estate investor.

DEALING WITH UNCLE SAM

The United States government offers special opportunities for individuals seeking shelter. If you have the time, the government has a program to help you. The United States Department of Housing and Urban Development (HUD) will be your best friend when you deal with government housing programs. Unless otherwise stated, the contact for more information on the following programs is:

Assistant Secretary for Housing
Federal Housing Commissioner
Department of Housing and Urban Development
Washington, DC 20410-8000

Urban Homesteading

Urban homesteading is a national program to revitalize neighborhoods and to reduce the number of properties owned by the federal government. These houses are frequently in need of repair. They are houses owned by HUD, the Veterans Administration (VA), and Farmers Home Administration (FmHA). These government agencies acquire the properties through the default of the original owner.

This program favors low-income buyers. As an urban homesteader, you must agree to live in the property for at least five years. Within three years, you must bring the property up to local code requirements. The rehab work can be done by you or a contractor. As the work is being done, you must allow periodic inspections of the property. When these requirements are met, you will receive fee simple title to the property.

The program calls the transfer fee nominal. The fee may vary in amount; check with HUD for complete details on the current status of the program. Since these properties will probably need work, you have the opportunity to build sweat equity. The acquisition cost is very low and the potential for homemade equity is good. If you don't want to make repairs to your first home, the program is still worth looking into. Not all the properties need extensive renovation; some may just be vacant, abandoned properties.

Joint Venture for Affordable Housing

This is a program aimed at creating affordable home ownership, especially for first-time buyers. By regulatory reform, elimination of red tape, and the use of creative construction techniques, the program encourages affordable housing. The program involves builders, developers, and local governments. This program also provides assistance and incentives to stimulate affordable housing.

Counseling for Home Buyers, Homeowners, and Tenants

This is a HUD program to counsel home buyers, homeowners, and tenants. HUD approves agencies and private and public groups to counsel people in need of assistance. The subjects of consultation include budgeting, money management, buying a home, and maintaining a home. The services extend to referrals for financial assistance and other services. Counseling is available without a fee.

HUD offers many other programs related to home ownership and home buying. Contact the department for full details on all available programs.

THEIR LOSS IS YOUR GAIN

Properties foreclosed on by financial institutions offer a great opportunity. When a lender forecloses on a property, he wants to sell it as fast as possible. He is only concerned with recovering his investment in the property. This desire can result is some tremendous savings for the smart home shopper. There is a second advantage attached to these repossessed homes. Since the bank owns them, obtaining financing to buy the property may be very easy. The bank badly wants someone to buy the home. When the bank is sitting on a vacant property, it receives no monthly income. If you step up and assume the loan, you are providing the lender with cash flow. This may be accomplished with little to no down payment.

If you wait until these properties are advertised, the price will be at its highest. Lenders have many investors to whom they can sell their foreclosed properties. By the time they advertise a foreclosure sale, they have exhausted their normal channels for liquidating the property. This loss in time has cost the bank more money. When they advertise to the public, they will try to recover this lost income. You can get an inside track on these properties with a letter to the proper department at your local banks.

Call the banks in your area and ask for the name of the officer in charge of the disposition of foreclosed properties. Write the disposition officer a letter showing your interest in purchasing distressed properties. It may take some time before you receive any meaningful information, but at least your name is in the pool. When properties are being liquidated, you will have a chance at them before the public does. This gives you an edge on the purchase price.

In your letter, don't identify yourself as a first-time buyer. Avoid making reference to your inexperience in the real estate market, but stress the fact that you plan to occupy the property purchased. As a lender, the risk of default is much lower with an owner-occupant than it is with an investor. If bank officers have had to reclaim a house once, they don't want to foreclose on it again. Your position as an owner-occupant will give you some advantage over the average investor.

WORKING WITH ACCOUNTANTS AND LAWYERS

Accountants and lawyers work with clients planning to sell their homes and rental properties. Accountants frequently help clients who are preparing to sell their tax shelters. Lawyers dealing with divorce and bankruptcies are excellent sources of good real estate deals. Their clients are very motivated and may be willing to sell cheap.

A letter to these professionals can result in some very rewarding opportunities. If they know you are looking for a home, they may refer you to their clients in need of making a quick sale. This source of unadvertised housing can account for thousands of dollars in extra equity. When you write them, describe what you are looking for and your ability to act quickly. There are no guarantees in real estate, but the odds are good you will receive some special opportunities from these professional advisors.

AUCTIONS

Auctions are a known source of wholesale homes. When houses go on the auction block, they are often sold below appraised value. While this is a favorable market, it is difficult for the average buyer to participate in auctions. Auctioned deals typically require cash deposits and fast closings. Unless you have a pre-established line of credit, you will have a tough time with auctions. Auctions may be worth your time, but they are not usually suitable for first-time buyers.

THE HUNT AND PECK METHOD

Another good way to find super deals is to make contact with sellers *before they plan to sell*. To do this, you will have to perform extensive research. If you want to live in a particular area, mail a letter to every homeowner in the neighborhood. Tell them of your interest in buying a home in their area. This is a numbers game. If you mail to a hundred homes, the chances are good someone will be planning to sell in the near future.

When the potential seller receives your letter, he will contact you before listing his home with a broker. If nothing else, you may save the cost of a brokerage commission. This tactic can produce very lucrative offerings. When people first plan to sell, they may not be aware of their home's market value. If you can get to them before a broker does, you stand a chance to buy the property at less than appraised value.

MILITARY INFLUENCE

If you live in an area with a prominent military influence, you can cash in on the opportunity. Military personnel relocate at periodic intervals. Contacting these soon-to-be sellers can result in big savings. Send a letter to the local military base and request that it to be placed on their public bulletin board. In the letter, stress your interest in buying a home in the military town. When service people plan to relocate, they are interested in quick sales.

Your willingness to purchase a home will attract attention. If the person is being shipped out, a willing buyer is a welcome sight. Most bases will be happy to post your notice on the bulletin board. If you know of certain homes containing military personnel, direct mail your offer to the homeowners. The timing on this type of strategy is unpredictable, but the results can be very rewarding.

CASTING YOUR NET

Don't overlook the obvious. It can be very productive to place a classified advertisement to inform the public of your interest in buying a home. If you do this, be prepared for an onslaught of calls from brokers. You will receive numerous worthless calls, but you could fall into an outrageously good deal. Your ad will generate many types of calls. If you are willing to sort through the mass of inquiries, a classified ad can pull fast results.

Some of the callers will want top dollar for their homes. Many of the calls will be brokers hoping to get a commission from selling you a home. A few calls will offer the type of deal you are looking for. These calls make the ad and the effort worthwhile. If you can establish a pre-approved line of credit, your range of options expands.

If you have an approved loan, you can stress your ability to close quickly on selected properties. This type of wording will induce distressed callers to respond to your ad. They may be on the edge of foreclosure and willing to take a pay-off amount on the house. Even though they are losing their equity, they are acting to reduce the negative effect of a foreclosure on their credit rating. Many high-rolling investors make their living with these types of deals. As a first-time buyer, it will probably be a struggle for you to obtain a line of credit sufficient to purchase a home. If you can, you are in the driver's seat.

BUYING FROM BUILDERS IN TROUBLE

Builders occasionally get in over their heads. They begin building and run out of money, or they build a custom home only to have the deal fall through. When these situations arise, you can capitalize on the builder's plight. Most new homes are financed with construction loans. These loans require monthly interest payments on the principal loan amount. If a builder has to hold onto a vacant house he cannot sell, he is losing money every day.

Driving around subdivisions can turn up these hidden treasures. When you find a new house without occupants, you are on the trail to potential profits. If you see a house in a stalled stage of construction, you have a chance to make big bucks. A trip to the tax assessor's office will reveal the owner of the property. When you have the builder's name and address, mail him a letter of interest. Explain your willingness to negotiate the purchase of the property you found.

Builders under pressure will sell their product way below appraised value. The average new home has a 20% profit built into it for the builder. If the

builder's credit line is tied up, he will want to sell the house *quickly*. He knows that every day the house sits idle, his profit is shrinking. When you want a new home with built-in equity, this is a solid approach to take.

SUMMARY

Finding properties with exceptional values is worth your time. The methods for locating these properties are only limited by your imagination. The key to winning at this stage of the game is the spread between the purchase price and the appraised value. This value should be closely estimated before you purchase a property. You can learn to estimate property values on your own or you can depend on professionals for appraisal help.

Real estate brokers are capable of estimating a property's current market value. Brokers are not necessarily appraisers, but they are qualified to give an opinion of value. If the broker is working for you, as a buyer's broker, her opinion should be fairly accurate. If you want a more accurate valuation, consult a licensed appraiser. The appraiser will be able to give you a more precise estimate of the property's value. If you decide to invest in the services of an appraiser, engage one who is approved by your lender.

Hiring a lender-approved appraiser will save you money during the acquisition process. If the appraiser is on the bank's approved list, you will be able to use your appraisal for loan purposes. This will eliminate the need to pay for a second appraisal.

Turning your attention to overlooked opportunities can result in huge profits. By buying smart, you can see immediate equity gains. Remember, it will take a very long time for your monthly payments to create sizable equity. Making the right deal can be equivalent to earning a year's salary by signing the contract. This is serious money and deserves deliberate thought. Don't limit yourself to my suggestions; put on your thinking cap. Come up with unique ways to find your best deal. The deals are there for the taking. It's only a matter of finding them.

8

Going from Renter to Landlord

When you think of getting out of your apartment, your mind probably jumps to a single-family home. Single-family residences are the customary vision of home ownership. Even so, they are not the only choice for a first home. For the first-time buyer with vision, small, multi-family buildings offer lucrative possibilities. Living in a multi-family property is very different when you are the landlord than when you are the tenant.

Buying a multi-family property with up to four apartments is not much different procedurally from buying a single-family home. Down payment requirements and loan terms are essentially the same. The purchase price will be higher, but you will have rental income to offset the higher monthly payments. With some creative thought, you may be able to structure a deal in which your tenants pay for your first home. When you put your mind to it, small multi-family properties are an excellent choice for your first home.

Small, multi-family properties are classified as buildings with two to four apartments. These properties may be financed with residential mortgage loans. This means you can buy an income property with only a 5% down payment. To do so, you must agree to live in the property, but you are not committed to living in the building for a specific period of time. You could live there for a month and then move and convert the building to a straight income property.

When you live in the property, your tenants will pay a large percentage of your house payment. This is especially true of properties with four units. Let's look at how your ownership of a four-unit building might work out.

FOUR-UNIT EXAMPLE

You purchase the building for $185,000. The property is acquired with a 5% down payment and a thirty-year, fixed rate loan at 9.5%. Your monthly principal and interest payment is $1,477.80. The annual real estate taxes are $1,200. Your water and sewer expenses are $800 per year. Each apartment has individual heating and hot water facilities. Your annual maintenance is low, because you take care of the property. The yearly maintenance averages $1,000.

The building is very nice and in a desirable location. This reduces the vacancy rate. Your annual vacancy rate is equivalent to $1,500. The total annual expenses of the property, including debt service, equals approximately $22,233. The property has two three-bedroom units and two two-bedroom apartments.

You live in one of the two-bedroom apartments and lease the remaining apartments to tenants. The three-bedroom units command monthly rents of $600. The rented two-bedroom apartment pulls a monthly rent of $525. This is a total monthly income of $1,725 or an annual income of $20,700. When you take your total monthly cost and subtract your average rental income, your cost to live in the property is only $1,533 per year. That is less than $130 per month.

Think of what this example shows you. In this building, you have a nice place to live for only $130 per month. You enjoy tax benefits from owning the property as a home and as an income property. Your down payment is manageable and your long-term investment has great potential. When you compare this to buying a single-family home, there is no doubt which purchase makes the most financial sense. While the financial end of the deal is clear, there are other considerations.

The decision to graduate from tenant to landlord should not be taken lightly. Financially, the results of buying a multi-family building are very appealing. This appeal may be tainted by the responsibility of becoming a landlord. Landlording is not a bad business, but it is a job some people prefer not to do. Even with a small, multi-family property, the duties of being the landlord can be hard. First, we will look at all the advantages of buying an income property to live in. Then the disadvantages will be addressed. By the time you complete this chapter, you will have a good idea of whether landlording is for you.

THE FINANCING ADVANTAGES

When you buy a single-family home, your buying power is determined strictly by your income and debt ratios. So buying an income property can help you qualify for a larger mortgage. If the seller has tax returns on the building's performance for the last two years, the income from the property can be used to help qualify you. If there are poor records and no tax returns, the income will not be allowed for qualifying purposes.

The Vacancy Rate

When lenders calculate the allowable income for qualifying purposes, they have some set standards to follow. These standards differ in percentages, but they show some historical averages. An average vacancy rate is 5% of the property's gross income. If the building is in a tough area, the rate may be much higher. In very desirable locations, the rate could be lower. If the tax returns of the building show an actual vacancy rate, the lender may accept it. For your calculations in evaluating income properties, a 5% vacancy rate is a good average to work with.

Maintenance Expenses

The next variable is called a maintenance allowance. Typically, this will be around 10% of the building's gross income. The maintenance expenses from past tax returns will have some bearing on the rate used by your lender. If the building is old and equipped with outdated mechanical systems, the rate may be higher. If the property is fairly new, the rate may be set at 5%. When the owner is going to live in the property, lenders are more likely to use a lower maintenance rate.

Management Fees

Non-owner-occupied properties are assessed a management fee. This fee is generally figured as 10% of the gross income. Since you will be living in the building, you should not have to contend with a management allowance. If the building was being professionally managed during the time reported on the tax returns, the lender may allow more net income to be used for qualifying you.

Real Estate Taxes and Utilities

Utility expenses and real estate taxes will be deducted from the gross income. These figures are obtained from the tax assessor and tax returns. If the seller has receipts for each month's expenses, the lender should accept them. Any other known expenses will be deducted from the gross income. When the bottom line is reached, the lender will be looking at the net income of the property.

If the previous owner did not live in the building, the lender will adjust the income to allow for your use of one of the apartments. When all is said and done, the lender will allow the remaining income to count as additional income for your qualifying criteria. This extra income can make a big difference in what you are qualified to borrow.

DOWN PAYMENTS, CASH-RESERVES, AND EXPERIENCE

For down payments, the minimum requirement for conventional loans will be 5% of the purchase price. VA loans will allow a veteran to buy a small multi-family property with no down payment. You may be required to show evidence of your ability to manage the rental property. It is not unusual for the lender to require some proof of your ability to act as landlord for the building. The lender may also require you to have a cash reserve to balance any rental losses during the first six months of ownership. Meeting the requirements of a landlord can be done in many ways. Your loan officer will tell you exactly what you must document to be eligible for the loan.

Creative Financing

In some cases, a creative lender will allow a second mortgage, held by the seller, to act as your down payment. In small multi-family buildings, this opportunity is rare. It is a common procedure with buildings having more than four units, but they are financed as commercial properties. The differences between a residential and commercial loan are many. If you find a seller willing to hold a second mortgage, it is worth talking to your loan officer. When this option is allowed, you are able to buy the property with lower or no down payment.

If the seller is involved in the financing, pay particular attention to the terms of the financing. Be sure to have your attorney review the documents before signing them. As a mortgage holder, the seller could be motivated to reclaim the property at the first hint of default. Mortgages and note terms are not set by law; the note holder can place many conditions on your loan. Caution should always be observed, but it should be doubled when dealing with a non-commercial lender.

OTHER ADVANTAGES

Depending on the property's performance, you may be able to live in the dwelling for free. Some small multi-family properties are capable of supporting themselves. Unless the building has four apartments, it is unlikely you can live in the building without contributing to the monthly payment. Duplexes and triplexes are not apt to produce enough income to support the monthly expenses. While you may have to supplement the monthly payment, it is very possible to live for less than you ever imagined.

The Tax Advantage

Tax laws change too often to predict your exact results in this book. At present, there are several tax advantages to owning and living in a multi-family property. To determine how these advantages apply to you, consult a tax professional.

The Investment Advantage

Real estate ownership is adorned with the promise of annual appreciation. The annual appreciation of real estate is determined by a percentage of the property's existing value. Buying an income property offers a major advantage in this category. The income property will cost more to purchase than a single-family home. This increased cost is offset by the rental income produced by the property. While for acquisition and monthly expenses these two factors equal out, they are not equal in appreciation.

Assume you buy a four-unit property for $185,000 and your friend buys a single-family home for $80,000. You had to make a larger down payment, but that was applied to the purchase of the property. Even though you had a higher expense in acquisition, it is reflected in equity. Your net monthly payments are equal to your friend's. In reality, your net payments could be much less than those of the single-family dwelling owner. Now look at what happens to each investment at the end of five years with an annual appreciation rate of 7%.

Your friend's house will be worth about $113,400. His investment has grown to show a profit of $33,400. Your income property will be worth more than $262,200. Your investment showed a profit of $77,200 in the same period of time. Each of you shared the same cost of ownership during the five years, but your investment produced $43,800 more than your friend's. By having your tenants pay for much of your mortgage, you win with appreciation.

When the time comes to sell your first home, the income property will offer another investment advantage. If you maintain the property and manage it well, the building will be desirable to investors. Your potential purchasers will include investors as well as owner-occupants. This expands your base of potential purchasers and increases your odds for a quick and profitable sale.

DISADVANTAGES OF OWNING MULTI-FAMILY PROPERTY

Financing Disadvantages

The higher sales price of a multi-family property can require you to have a larger cash down payment than for a single-family home. The need for the larger down payment is a disadvantage. The increased down payment is not a waste of money; it applies to the purchase price and increases your equity. Increasing your equity is fine if you have the money, but if you don't, the larger down payment can be a hardship.

If your lender requires a demonstration of your ability to manage the property, that can be a disadvantage. You are not required to have any special ability when buying a single-family home. Cash reserve requirements are another potential disadvantage. Some lenders may require a certain amount of cash reserve to protect against losses in the first months of ownership with an income property. This is not a factor with a single-family home. Some loan regulations require you to have a cash reserve to buy a house, but the amount is much smaller.

Some financial institutions may frown upon making loans for income property. A lender who is anxious to loan on a house may shy away from a multi-family property. This is especially true if you are trying to use the building's income to help you qualify for the loan.

Disadvantages of Rental Income

It is hard to find a disadvantage to receiving additional income. A possible disadvantage is the risk of the rental income failing to come in. If you are plagued with vacancies or bad tenants, the loss of income can crush you financially. When you are dependent on rental income to make your payments, life can be quite stressful during spells without rental income.

With good management, a long-term lack of rental income is unlikely but possible. This must be considered a disadvantage. In a worst case scenario, you could lose your home from the lack of regular rental income. With a house, you are not counting on rental income to make your payments. The lack of income is the only real disadvantage related to additional income.

Tax Disadvantages

I am not aware of any disadvantages to living in a multi-family property when it comes to income taxes.

Investment Disadvantages

Investment disadvantages are present with income properties. Normally, they are outweighed by the advantages, but to be fair, you must acknowledge them. The first of these disadvantages is the potential for the property's decline in physical condition. When you buy a house, yours is the only family living in it. You will take care of the home and ensure its growth in value. With a multi-family building, you lose some control over this critical aspect of your investment.

Bad Tenants

As you rent your apartments, the tenants could destroy them. They could steal your appliances and move out in the middle of the night owing you rent. They could put holes in the walls or damage your mechanical systems. Their abuse might ruin your floor coverings or plumbing fixtures. The potential for damage is extensive, and the threat of loss is real.

If the tenants are properly screened before moving in, you eliminate many of the risks. Since you will be living in the building, you should have a good idea of the quality of your tenants. If a problem arises, being on-site will allow you to correct the problem promptly. Nevertheless, you cannot ignore the possibility of destruction caused by the tenants. Repairing your damaged property can become very expensive. This is a loss of out-of-pocket money you may not have. If the repairs are not made, the property value will decline rapidly.

Slower Appreciation Rates

An income property may not appreciate as much as a single-family home. The location of multi-family properties has a heavy influence on annual appreciation. While your building should show an average appreciation, a single-family home has a better chance for a higher than average appreciation. Even if the income property does not exhibit as high a rate of appreciation, it may still beat the single-family home. Since appreciation is based on existing value, the income property has an advantage.

The income property should be worth substantially more than a single-family home. When appreciation rates are applied to each property, the multi-family building should show a higher rate of return. Let's look at an example of this situation. Your multi-family property is worth $185,000, and your friend's house is worth $80,000. The appreciation rate for your building is 7%. The rate for the home is 11%. At the end of five years, your building will have produced an equity gain of about $77,200. Your friend's house has enjoyed a higher rate of appreciation, but it only showed a profit of about $58,300. Even with the disadvantage of a lower appreciation rate, your property won the race by about $19,000.

Sales Appeal
When it is time to sell your apartment building, you could be at a disadvantage. You have the advantage of appealing to owner-occupants and investors, but you are disadvantaged by the higher sales price. The higher price and down payment requirement will narrow the margin of qualified buyers. The income of the property should offset the higher monthly payments, but the down payment could remain a problem. Some buyers will have no interest in multi-family properties. These are buyers who might show strong attention to a single-family home and none to your income property. This is a risk you must take if you decide to become a landlord.

PERSONAL DISADVANTAGES TO LANDLORDING

This group of disadvantages may well be the most important for you to ponder. You will deal with these adversities on a daily basis. They are the primary reason more people do not buy income properties. Making an honest evaluation of your

feelings towards these points will be the deciding factor in your decision on buying a multi-family property.

Living with Your Tenants
Living in the same building with your tenants can be troublesome. You have the advantage of being close by in case of emergencies, and you are able to monitor your tenants' activities easily. This very advantage is also a disadvantage. The tenants not only know where you live, they have easy access to you. If they have a complaint, they will be right there knocking on your door. They may even stop you when you are going from your car to your apartment. There is no opportunity for you to create a buffer zone.

Investors who do not live in their buildings have an advantage over the owner-occupant. When a tenant calls, the investor can stall the conversation by arranging a time to meet and discuss the problem in person. This gives the investor time to think and develop a plan. When an irate tenant catches you in the yard, there is no time to reflect on the problem. You are forced to deal with it immediately. This leaves the door open for you to make a bad decision.

Having the risk of angry tenants at your door is more than some people can deal with. This is easily avoided if you manage the building properly. Happy tenants will not ruin your dinner by banging on your door and screaming. There will undoubtedly be times when the tenants will approach you. If you are uncomfortable with the idea of dealing with the tenants, landlording is not for you.

Lack of Solitude
Many people seek home ownership to escape apartment life. As the owner and occupant of an income property, you will not enjoy the solitude of a single-family home. There will be times when your tenants will get on your nerves. Their stereo will be too loud, their car's exhaust will be noisy, or their overall presence will annoy you. This kind of problem is usually avoided with a single-family home. The reward of rental income and a good investment will go a long way in extending most people's

patience. If these benefits don't seem adequate for the inconveniences associated with multi-family living, don't buy income property.

Getting Too Friendly

Living in the same building with your tenants can make it difficult to maintain a business relationship. The tenants may wish to become friends with you. This attachment must be avoided. If you get too friendly, you lose control as the landlord. A principal element to successful landlording is control. If you give that up, you will not be an effective property manager.

The Flurry of Phone Calls

When you have a vacant apartment, you must advertise for new tenants. These ads can produce up to fifty or more phone calls in a single week. Many of the callers will be curiosity callers. They will ask numerous questions and decide the apartment is not right for them. Your personal time will be eroded by the mass of phone inquires. Again, with good management, the need for filling vacancies will not be a common occurrence.

Showing Apartments

When vacancies occur, the only way to fill them is by showing them to prospective tenants. This is another time-consuming and frustrating part of the business. Many of the appointments made by interested parties will not be kept. You will wait around to show an apartment to a would-be tenant who never shows up. After a while, "no-shows" can become aggravating. When the people keep their appointments, you must become a salesperson.

Vacancies cost you money, and it is your job to fill them quickly with quality tenants. There is much more to showing an apartment successfully than unlocking the door. You should describe the features and benefits of the dwelling to the prospective tenants. Make them want to live in your apartment. If you are self-conscious, this part of the job can be disconcerting. If you are paranoid that every stranger is a criminal, you will not do well as a rental agent.

There is a small but real danger in showing your property. The interested parties could have criminal intent. They may inspecting the property for a future burglary. These circumstances are rare, but you should be aware that the potential exists. These risks can be lowered with proper pre-qualifying requirements. When a caller asks to see your property, get a name and phone number. Call the individual back to verify the appointment. This call will tell you whether the caller gave you his real phone number. Call directory assistance and ask for the phone number of the individual.

Directory assistance should have a listing of all active numbers. It is possible the phone is not listed in the name of your caller, but it is worth checking. When people arrive to view your apartments, write down their license plate numbers and a brief description of their car. If something does happen later, this information can help police check for suspects. When showing the apartment, arrange for someone else to know you are showing one of the units. If anything goes wrong, your assistant can notify the police.

The Legal Side of Landlording

Good paperwork is essential to successful landlording. You will need more than leases. There are sample forms at the back of the chapter to illustrate the paperwork you may require as a landlord. If you buy a multi-family property, consult with an attorney to obtain the documents needed to run your building. When you talk with your attorney, ask for a full explanation of your obligations as a landlord. Tenant's rights and rental laws vary from state to state. It is important for you to be aware of what is required of you.

Maintenance

To keep your property profitable, you may have to do much of the routine maintenance yourself. This could encompass everything from emergency plumbing repairs to repainting apartments. If you are not able to perform these functions, allow for professional maintenance fees in your income projections.

Negative Cash Flow

Negative cash flow is something you never want to experience in large doses. If you are unable to weather a financial storm of repairs or vacancies, an income property is a risky investment. You should have reserve capital or a line of credit you can depend on to counteract unforeseen expenses. Without a cash cushion, you could take a damaging fall into financial despair.

THE BALANCE SHEET

Now you have a good view of what is involved with buying a multi-family property for your first home. There are many advantages to this investment strategy—if you have a personality suited to landlording. The financial rewards can be astonishing, and the personal sacrifices are what you make them. If you have digested this information, you should have a good feel for your interest in pursuing an income property. While there is not enough room in a single chapter to describe landlording fully, you have gotten a solid overview of the job description.

Many of you will have decided rental property is not the best choice for your first home. This is not an unusual conclusion; it takes a special type of individual to be a property manager. Single-family homes appeal to more people than multi-family dwellings. If you have decided against rental property, you have eliminated one of the possible confusions of your first real estate purchase. Without some knowledge of how income property works, it can present a temptation to first-time buyers.

If you are interested in buying a multi-family building, you should investigate landlording further. There are books available dedicated solely to the practice of property management. Before making a multi-family purchase, you owe it to yourself to invest your time in gaining a full understanding of your responsibilities and liabilities as a landlord. With the right combination, rental property can make an excellent first home.

TENANT RENTAL APPLICATION

Name _____

Social Security # _____ Home Phone _____

PREVIOUS ADDRESSES (If at current address for less than 2 years)

Address _____ From _____ to _____

Landlord's name _____ Phone _____

Reason for moving _____

Address _____ From _____ to _____

Landlord's name _____ Phone _____

Reason for moving _____

Driver's license # _____ State _____

Vehicle license # _____ State _____

Car make _____ Model _____ Year _____

CREDIT REFERENCES

Name _____ Account # _____

Address _____

Name _____ Account # _____

Address _____

Name _____ Account # _____

Address _____

Name, address, and phone number of nearest relative not living with you

_____

Names, addresses, and phone numbers of two personal references not related to you

_____

_____

Names of all people planning to reside in your rental unit

_____

OTHER PERTINENT INFORMATION: _____

_____

I give my permission for the landlord or his agent to verify information in this application and to investigate my credit standing. This permission is extended to _____.

_____

Prospective Tenant   Date

30-DAY NOTICE TO TERMINATE TENANCY

To _____, tenant in possession:

Please be advised, you are hereby required within thirty days from this date to vacate and deliver possession of the premises now held by you, being those premises situated in the city of

_____, county of _____,

state of _____, commonly known as _____.

This notice is intended for the purpose of terminating the agreement by which you now hold possession of the above-described property. Should you fail to comply with this order, legal proceedings will be levied against you to recover possession of the property. In addition, the agreement by which you presently hold the property will be forfeited. It will be the intent to recover rents and damages for the period of the unlawful detention.

Please be advised that your rent on said premises is due and payable up to and including the date of termination of your tenancy under this notice.

Dated this _____ day of _____, 19_____.

_____

Owner

PROOF OF SERVICE

I, the undersigned, being of legal age, declare under penalty of perjury that I served the thirty-day notice to terminate tenancy, of which this is a true copy, on the above-mentioned tenant in possession in the following manner:

Executed on _____, 19_____, at _____.

By: _____

Title: _____

RENTAL POLICY FORM

GENERAL RULES AND REGULATIONS FOR TENANTS

1. Keep all areas clean.

2. Do not disturb other people's peace and quiet.

3. Do not alter the dwelling.

4. Park only in assigned parking spaces.

5. Keep the parking area clean and free of oil drippings.

6. Do not repair motor vehicles on the premises.

7. Owners may inspect the dwelling with 24 hours' verbal notice.

8. Owners may have reasonable access to have work done on the dwelling.

9. Owners or their agent may show the dwelling to prospective tenants or purchasers at reasonable times, with 24 hours' verbal notice.

10. Use of a water bed requires written permission from the landlord.

11. Tenant is required to pay all costs of repairs or damage, including drain stoppages they or their guests cause.

12. Tenants shall maintain adequate heat in their dwelling at all times to prevent plumbing from freezing.

13. Tenants shall provide Owners with a punch list of any existing items that are damaged, missing, or in need of repair within five days of taking possession of the property.

14. Pets are allowed only by written permission of the landlord.

15. Violation of any part of these requirements or the conditions of the lease, or nonpayment of rent as agreed, shall be cause for eviction and all legal action allowed by law.

NOTICE TO PAY RENT OR QUIT

To _____, tenant in possession:

Please be advised, your rent is now due and payable on the premises held and occupied by you, being

those premises situated in the city of _____, county of

_____, state of _____, commonly known as

_____.

Your account is delinquent in the amount of $_____,

being the rent for the period from _____ to _____.

You are required to pay said rent in full within _____ days or remove yourself from and deliver
up possession of the above-mentioned premises. If this order is not complied with, legal proceedings
will be instituted against you to recover possession of said premises, to declare the forfeiture of all
agreements between us and to recover rents and damages, including court costs and attorney's fees,
according to the terms of our agreement.

Dated this _____ day of _____, 19_____.

_____
Owner

PROOF OF SERVICE

I, the undersigned, being of legal age, declare under penalty of perjury that I served this notice to pay
or quit, of which this is a true copy, on the above-mentioned tenant in possession as follows:

_____

_____

Executed on _____, 19_____, at _____.

By: _____

Title: _____

30-DAY NOTICE TO PERFORM COVENANT

To _____, tenant in possession:

Please be advised, you have violated the following covenant(s) in our agreement:

_____

_____

You are hereby required within _____ days to perform the aforesaid covenant or deliver possession

of the premises now held by you, being those premises situated in the city of _____,

county of _____, state of _____, commonly known as _____.

If you fail to do so, legal proceedings will be brought against you to recover said premises and all restitution allowed by law.

This notice is intended to require performance of the afore-mentioned covenant. It is not intended to terminate or forfeit the agreement under which you occupy said premises.

Dated this _____ day of _____, 19_____.

_____

Owner

PROOF OF SERVICE

I, the undersigned, being of legal age, declare under penalty of perjury that I served this notice to pay or quit, of which this is a true copy, on the above-mentioned tenant in possession as follows:

_____

_____

Executed on _____, 19_____, at _____.

By: _____

Title: _____

LEASE

This agreement is between _____, Owners,

and _____, Tenants, for a dwelling located at

_____, unit number _____. Tenants agree to lease this dwelling

for a term of _____, beginning _____, and ending _____, for

$_____ per _____, payable in advance on _____.

Rent shall be paid to _____. Payments shall be mailed to _____

_____, at _____. The first _____ rent for this

dwelling is $_____. The entire sum of this lease is $_____. This deposit is refundable if Tenants comply with this lease and leave the dwelling clean and undamaged. If Tenants intend to move at the end of this lease, they agree to give Owners notice, in writing, at least thirty days before the lease expires. A deposit of $_____ will be required for two keys. It will be refunded to the Tenants when both keys are returned to the Owners. Owners will refund all deposits due within ten days after Tenants have moved out completely and returned the keys. Only the following persons are to live in the above-mentioned dwelling: _____

_____.

Without Owners' prior written permission, no other persons may live in the dwelling and no pets shall be admitted to the dwelling, even temporarily. The dwelling may not be sublet or used for business purposes. Use of the following is included in the rent at Tenants' own risk: _____.

Tenants agree to the following: 1) To keep all areas clean. 2) Not to disturb other people's peace and quiet. 3) Not to alter the dwelling without first obtaining the Owners' written permission. 4) To park in an assigned parking space. 5) To keep the parking area clean and free of oil drippings. 6) Not to repair motor vehicles on the premises. 7) To allow Owners to inspect the dwelling with 24 hours' verbal notice. 8) To allow the Owners reasonable access to have work done on the dwelling. 9) To allow the Owners, or their agent, to show the dwelling to prospective tenants or purchasers at reasonable times, with 24 hours' verbal notice. 10) Not to use a water bed without written permission from the Owners. 11) To pay all costs of repairs or damages, including drain stoppages, they or their guests cause. 12) To maintain adequate heat in the dwelling at all times to prevent plumbing from freezing. 13) To inform the Owners of any defects or material problems that may cause damage to the property. Violation of any part of this agreement, or nonpayment of rent as agreed, shall be cause for eviction and all legal action allowed by law. The Owners reserve the right to seek any legal means to collect monies owed to them. The prevailing party shall recover reasonable attorney's fees.

SPECIAL TERMS OR CONDITIONS

_____

_____

Tenants hereby acknowledge that they have read this agreement, understand the entire agreement, agree to the entire agreement, and have been given a copy of the agreement.

IF YOU DO NOT UNDERSTAND THIS DOCUMENT, CONSULT AN ATTORNEY.
THIS IS A LEGAL, BINDING DOCUMENT.

Owner	Date	Tenant	Date
Owner	Date	Tenant	Date
Witness	Date	Witness	Date

9
Making the Decision

Making a quick decision in real estate can be both essential and devastating. When you find a particularly good value, someone will want to buy it fast. If you want the property, you must act to beat the competition to it. In the excitement of the deal, you could make some very costly mistakes. Defining what you want to buy and setting a price you are willing to pay will help to make a sound buying decision.

Once you have found the perfect home, your emotions can take control. With emotions running high, your logic may be lacking. This is when most buyers make mistakes. Rushing to get the property under contract is dangerous. It may be necessary to act quickly, but you are not obligated to make quick decisions without prudence. Making the proper preparations will reduce your risks. Before you find yourself in a compromising position, set guidelines for your buying decision.

With your guidelines established, you will not make negligent errors. There is no reasonable way to avoid becoming emotionally involved in buying your first home, but being prepared will reduce your risk of major mistakes. Many elements are involved in your buying strategy and decision. What follows is an evaluation of each of these elements and how you can control them.

HOW MUCH CAN YOU AFFORD FOR YOUR FIRST HOME?

Chapter 1 showed you how to determine how much house you can afford. Using the information in Chapter 1, decide what you are willing to spend for your first home. Most people will establish this from a monthly payment they are comfortable making. Many times, people qualify for a higher mortgage than they are willing to pay. This is an area worth discussing.

If you are working with a broker, the broker will pre-qualify you for financing before showing you homes. This helps the broker make the best use of her time. It is senseless for a broker to show you homes you cannot qualify to buy. It is also better for you not to look at homes beyond your means. When buyers see a home they love but cannot afford, they are unable to settle for a different house. This emotional upheaval is not necessary.

It is simple to determine what amount of money lenders will agree to loan you for a house. As discussed in Chapter 1, setting your own budget is more difficult. Follow the advice in Chapter 1 to define clearly how much you are willing to spend for your home. A new home is wonderful, but it is not worth giving up everything else you enjoy in life. A maximum house payment can prevent you from taking vacations, pursuing hobbies, and enjoying other activities requiring discretionary income.

When brokers and bankers qualify you, they don't examine your preference for discretionary income. They work with fixed ratios to determine what loan amount you are qualified to borrow. If you spend $50 a month for a fitness club membership, the bank does not care. This is a voluntary expense you can terminate at will. They will not treat this monthly payment as a debt, but you should, if the club membership is important to you. Many discretionary commitments fall into this category. Your life insurance, health insurance, and car insurance are good examples. These are commitments you want to continue — outlays that the lender will not account for.

When you look at houses, take your Essential Features form with you. This form will serve as your guideline in finding the right house. You will be able to check quickly for features you want. When you get to the point of making an offer, these guidelines will prove very helpful. When you combine the guidelines of the Essential Features form with your Wish List, it will be hard to go wrong in your home-buying decision.

DECIDING ON A SUITABLE LOCATION

When you have decided what price range you are looking for, you must decide *where* you are willing to live. This process can be divided into three categories. When making your decision, select and classify different locations. Prioritize them as first, second, and third choices. Doing this will eliminate wasted time looking at homes in undesirable locations.

Rural, Urban, or City?

Do you want to live in a rural, urban, or city environment? If you are contemplating country living, how large does the building lot need to be? If you have horses and require a minimum of five acres, there is no point in looking at homes with only one acre of land. When you want to be close to schools and shopping, a gorgeous house in the country will not please you. Without your established guidelines, you could become enamored by the charm of the country estate. This blind passion could cause you to make a purchase commitment you will soon regret.

WATCH OUT FOR EMOTIONS

Emotions have a strong influence on human reactions. When buying real estate, it is essential to keep your emotions under control and in perspective. Your written guidelines will accomplish this task. First, decide on the type of location you want to live in. Then, define the parameters for the land surrounding your home.

First-time buyers without a focus will often look at any property they can afford. They may jump from townhouses to country estates. This is not only confusing, it is non-productive. Pinpoint the features you desire in your new home's location. Buying the perfect home in the city will not satisfy your urge to plant a large vegetable garden. This type of personal desire is frequently overlooked in the excitement of house-hunting.

It is very easy to become infatuated with a home and forget that you want to get away from sirens and traffic noise. When you are looking at a home, these requirements will not be at the top of your mental list of things to look for. By having the guidelines, you will have a written reminder of items to assess at each property you see. Experienced real estate investors know the value of a written business plan. When they shop for a new investment, they know what they are looking for. When the investor finds the right property, he is able to act quickly to secure it. As a first-time buyer, you should take a lesson from successful investors and draft your own buying plan.

STICK TO A PLAN

There are so many factors involved in buying your first home that it is almost impossible to remember them all. When you couple this confusion with intense emotions, you may forget important requirements of your purchase. By following your guidelines, you will be prompted to remember your vital fundamentals for purchasing a home. This is good business, and it will protect you from making a mistake you have to live with for years to come.

LOT SIZE

Lot size is something many people never consider until after they have committed themselves to buying a house. Once the excitement of living in a new home wears off, you may decide that a quarter-acre lot is not large enough to make you happy. The tiny back yard of your new townhouse may be a source of aggravation every time you cook out. Predetermining your land requirements will narrow the field of potential properties for your inspection. By setting parameters for your purchase, your house-hunting quest will be more efficient and more fun.

PICKING THE RIGHT STYLE

What style of home do you want? When a majority of first-time buyers are asked this question, they don't have an answer. The husband might express a desire for a colonial, while the wife wants a Cape Cod. The colonial is a two-story home, and the Cape Cod is a one-and-a-half story residence. Some buyers will answer the question with a question. They may ask what styles are available. When you don't know what you want, it will be very difficult to find it.

Should your first home be a ranch or a colonial? Average home buyers are familiar with these two styles of homes, but many have not considered the advantages each style offers. There are so many types of houses available that picking the ideal style may be difficult. To narrow the field, you can start with the basics. Do you want your home to have stairs? If you are against having stairs in your home, you have eliminated most styles. Cape Cods, Tudors, colonials, and most contemporaries have stairs.

Your decision to buy a home without stairs points you in the direction of ranch-style homes. This makes the process easier but not easy. Knowing you want all your living space on one floor is one thing; knowing *how* you want the exterior to look is another. Ranches can have many looks from the exterior. Your one-level home could be styled in a Spanish design, a contemporary look, or one of many other more traditional configurations. What do you want the house to look like? Should it have vinyl siding or wood siding? Do you want the home to have a porch or a garage? Answering these questions before seriously seeking a home is very helpful. Why bother looking at two-story homes if you have your mind set against stairs?

How to Decide on a Style

How should you decide on a house style? The simple way is to look through books of house plans. These books will have floor plans and illustrations of different house styles. A few hours with a variety of house-plan books will help you decide on the styles you appreciate. Then work through your choices and prioritize them. The illustrations will show you how the same house looks with different roof styles. The roof of a home can change its appearance dramatically.

Roof Designs

Two straight-up two-story homes can have the same floor plan but with a different roof design, each takes on an entirely different look. Some of the roof designs to choose from are gable, gambrel, mansard, hip, and saltbox. Any of these roofs can transform two homes with identical floor plans into completely different-looking houses. Picking the style of your home will take time and careful thought. While it may seem taxing, much of this work will be fun.

Full-Scale Models

You can ride through neighborhoods to see how the different house styles look in full scale. This preliminary research will reduce your time in finding the house of your dreams. It also protects you from buying a house only to find a style you like better a month later. Choosing your favorite style should be followed with planning the specifications you want in your home.

MAKING A SPEC SHEET

When you begin to look at houses, it will be hard to remember every feature you would like the house to have. Unless you have a specification sheet to work with, you may buy a home with important features missing. To help you compile your specifications in one place, use your Wish List and Essential Features form. The Wish List will require you to think. You must decide what you want your new house to offer. As you make these decisions, you will fill in the blanks on the form. Taking the house one room at a time is the best way to define your minimum requirements.

As you read through the options on the Wish List, you will think of items you want in the home. Filling out the form will prompt you to make decisions now, instead of while you are making an offer to purchase the house. Defining your buying criteria will be much easier when you have plenty of time and are not under pressure to purchase the perfect home. In the heat of negotiations, many items slip through the cracks. Don't allow yourself to miss out on the features you desire most in a home.

HOW IS YOUR MEMORY?

The Basic Housing Needs form will assist you in setting your goals for major elements in your new home. The Basic Housing Desires form will enable you to identify very specific features you have your heart set on. You might be surprised how many buyers inspect a house and cannot recall what type of heat it has. As a broker, I have shown homes and heard potential buyers who could not remember what color the carpet was. Other buyers have drawn a complete blank when asked if they liked the wainscoting in the dining room. The inability to recall features in a home dictates a need for a checklist. Your Needs form will enable you to check for specific attributes you want in a home. By taking your Needs and Desires forms with you on showings, you can make notes as you tour the property.

NEIGHBORHOOD CONVENIENCES

This is a subject most home buyers never consider until they purchase a home. Is it important for you to be in a certain school district? Are biking trails or nearby playgrounds high on your priority list? Will the location of shopping facilities or bus lines make a difference to you? Make a list of any of these types of questions to ask the seller or his agent. List your questions on the Decision Guidelines form so they won't be forgotten.

If you stumble onto the otherwise perfect property, these considerations will not be remembered. Can you imagine buying the apparently perfect property, only to find that your child must attend an undesirable school? This type of personal preference may not be critical, but it contributes to your family's overall happiness. There is no reason to buy a home that does not satisfy your minimum needs, but you must know what those minimum needs are.

REAL ESTATE TAXES

Real estate taxes can have a powerful impact on your monthly payment. Local taxing authorities frequently have tax rates differing from those of the adjoining tax jurisdiction. The fluctuation in tax rates from community to community should be considered in your selection process. Ask your broker or the local tax assessors for the tax rates in the areas you are considering. You may be surprised at how much difference there will be in your house payment from one boundary to the next.

Real estate taxes are an expense you will be obligated to pay as a property owner. I have seen situations when driving a few miles could reduce the property taxes by more than 40%. This type of savings could mean the difference between getting a house you love and a house you can live with. With the impact of real estate taxes on your monthly payment, it will be well worth your time to establish the tax rate in various locations. Driving a few extra miles to work could save you over a hundred dollars a month.

COVENANTS AND RESTRICTIONS

Are you planning to do anything special with your home after purchasing it? Do you want to fence the yard for your child to play in? Will you be running your business out of the house? Do you drive a company vehicle home from work? These are things you may take for granted, but you should not. Covenants and restrictions can limit what you are allowed to do with your property. These restrictions are designed to protect the integrity and value of the neighborhood, but they can ruin your plans. Don't wait until you own the property to discover you cannot follow through with your dreams.

Depending on the restrictions, you may not be allowed to park a commercial vehicle in your driveway. Your travel trailer or motor home might have to be parked in a common compound. The exterior of your home may not be able to be altered in any way. Will you be happy in a place where you cannot choose the color of your home if you decide to paint it? These restrictions are recorded for public inspection. They can be found in property deeds and subdivision filings. Your broker should be willing to provide copies of these documents upon request.

If the broker is uncooperative, you can investigate the covenants and restrictions yourself. A visit to the Registry of Deeds will unveil the rules and regulations pertaining to any proposed purchase. Municipal employees are generally very helpful in directing you to these recorded documents. If you are unable to secure the information, your attorney will be familiar with the deed and subdivision examination process.

Covenants and restrictions can inhibit a wide variety of items and activities. Never take these restrictions for granted. Always investigate any restrictions that may apply to your purchase before making an ironclad commitment. Most covenants and restrictions are found on properties located in subdivisions and developments. If you are buying rural property, there may not be any restrictions. Another source of restrictions is zoning. Depending on your personal circumstances, zoning may be something else worthy of your attention.

ZONING

Zoning can have untold effects on a property's value. With the right zoning, a home's value can skyrocket. If you buy a home with business zoning at a residential price, you could be sitting on a future fortune. Conversely, zoning can destroy your dreams if you are not aware of the restrictions caused by the zoning laws.

Let's say you are interested in buying a small, multi-family income property. You tour a property for sale by the owner and like it. The property is an older home, divided into three apartments. You see an opportunity to buy the property and let the tenants pay most of your mortgage payment. The property is more expensive than what you were planning to spend, but the rental income offsets this factor.

You investigate the structural and mechanical systems of the property. As far as you can tell, the building is in excellent condition. You are dealing directly with the seller and set a meeting to cut a deal. The seller seems fair enough, and you make a deal and buy the property. Your qualifications allowed you to purchase the property without using the building's income for qualification purposes. Your first hint of a problem is the appraiser's note about the use of the property.

The appraiser advised the lender that the property may not be zoned for multi-family use. In all the excitement, you didn't notice this statement during the closing procedures. The bank was not concerned because you qualified for the property as a single-family residence. The lender couldn't care less if the building is a legal multi-family dwelling.

Once your transaction is complete, the tax assessor pays you a visit to update his records. You sense a problem and ask the tax assessor if one exists. He refuses to comment on any problem, but you feel something is not right. The next day, you get a phone call from the code enforcement office. They are inquiring about the use of the property. Answering honestly, you explain the property is a triplex. This is where it all hits the fan.

The code enforcement office tells you the property is not zoned for multi-family use, and you must convert the property to a single-family dwelling. This new information shocks you. It never crossed your mind that the property might have been being used for an illegal application. The code enforcement office allows you a specific period of time to cease your rental endeavors. This demand will put a severe crunch in your cash flow.

When you remove the two tenants, your house payment is a serious burden. Due to the zoning laws, you have no choice in the matter. Since you didn't make special provisions in your purchase contract, you have no recourse against the seller. The seller never told you the house was a legal triplex and you never asked. The result of this problem could force you to sell your home, or even worse, lose it to foreclosure.

Zoning has many effects on real estate. You will do well to establish the zoning requirements before seeking a home. The zoning laws can prohibit you from operating a business in your home, and they can restrict many other uses of the property. The multi-family example is not rare. As a broker, I have encountered numerous properties operating in violation of zoning laws. If you want to use your home for something other than a residence, check the zoning laws carefully first, before you buy.

PROPERTY OWNER ASSOCIATION FEES

Are you willing to pay an association fee to live in a selected area? Many developments require a fee from every homeowner to offset the cost of certain services and other amenities. The services may include trash removal, road maintenance, and groundskeeping. The amenities could be a tennis court, swimming pool, or playground. Seeing these attractive options could spur you to commit to a house in the development. When you are ready to purchase the home and find out about the fee, you might find yourself in turmoil.

To avoid this confusion and possible disappointment, make your decision on association fees now. Decide how much you are willing to pay and what must be included in the fee. For example, ask yourself what you would be willing to pay for the use of a pool and fitness center. Lay out these scenarios now and save yourself the stress when you fall in love with a house requiring association fees.

FINANCING

When making an offer to purchase real estate, the financing terms are typically included. If you are sitting in a restaurant with your broker and writing the offer, do you know what type of financing to specify? For most people, this is a critical element of home ownership. As you will see in Chapter 11, there are countless options when it comes to financing.

After reading Chapter 11, you will have a broad knowledge of the most common types of residential financing. Once you know enough to ask the right questions, talk with your loan officer. Ask the loan officer to pre-qualify you for the type of financing you want. The lender will be able to give you a full disclosure on the various financing plans available. The type of loan you want could affect the type of house for which you should be looking.

Financing designed to help low-income buyers may restrict the features a house may have to be eligible for the financing. If the home has too many bathrooms or luxury features, it may not be possible for you to finance it. If you are going to finance the home through the Veterans Administration, the seller is required to pay points at closing. This cost can amount to several thousand dollars and may affect the price you offer for the property.

By talking with your loan officer now, you will be prepared when the time comes to write a purchase offer. You will be reasonably sure of your buying power and will know how you want the financing contingency worded. Once you have established these criteria, include them on your Guidelines form. When the broker asks you what kind of financing to specify in the offer, you will be able to quote the exact wording you want.

CONTINGENCIES

Contingencies are your safety net. With the proper wording, contingencies protect you from the loss of your earnest money deposit and a possible lawsuit. Since most brokers will be working for the seller, they may not be too helpful with your contingencies. It is up to you to decide what forms of protection you need. A buyer's broker or an attorney can help you list any possible contingencies.

Chapter 12 gives examples of contract contingencies and their purposes. After reading Chapter 12, jot down every contingency you can think of that might apply to your purchase. Then, meet with your attorney or buyer's broker and discuss the list with him. Ask for advice on other contingencies you should consider.

While you will presumably choose a house before every possible contingency clause can be designed, you can get a head start. Some contingencies should be standard language in your purchase offer. They include such matters as financing, inspections, title searches, and a host of other possibilities. Making a list of your known contingencies will ensure that they are not forgotten when your offer to purchase is written. Attach your list of standard contingencies to your Guidelines form for quick reference when preparing your offer.

SET YOUR CRITERIA

Defining your buying criteria is imperative to making a good investment in your first home. A few hours of preparation can save you years of frustration. Once you are actively engaged in negotiations for a prime property, you will be vulnerable to the emotional rush of realizing a long-held dream. Your excitement will consume you and push logic far back into another, foggier part of your brain. This temporary paralysis can cost you plenty if you fall into the buyer's blues trap.

When you have pre-defined your buying requirements, you will be able to muster control through trying times. Your written guidelines will counterbalance your brief loss of common sense. When you are under the spell of a broker, the guidelines will be your shield. If you make and stick to your buying guidelines, you will hedge your odds against a poor decision. Chapter 10 is going to train you in the art of professional negotiation. Before you use these negotiation tools, be sure to know your buying requirements. You never know when your most absurd offer may be accepted, and if it is accepted, you must honor the terms of your offer.

10
Playing Volleyball

Making your best deal on real estate can be compared to a volleyball game. When you make an offer to purchase, you are serving the ball into the seller's court. When you serve, you expect the seller to return the ball to your court, in the form of a counter offer. This repetitious volleying can go on for days. The seller will submit a counter offer, and you will counter with another offer. When the game is finished, you may have a contract to purchase your first home.

Once you have established your buying criteria, the negotiation stage will be critical to your success in owning a home. Strong negotiation skills are a gift to some and a learned trait for others. Professional salespeople have developed the ability to harness the power of negotiation. Since you will be likely to deal with these professional salespeople, you must understand negotiation strategies. If you are not able to recognize barter manipulations, you will pay too much for your property.

Understanding the methods of power negotiations will give you an edge in buying your first home. If you have natural talent, you can hone the skills into a very decisive tool. Buying your first house is a unique experience. You will never again buy a first home. If you are unwilling to invest your efforts in understanding the bargaining process, you will suffer in your acquisition.

There are two scenarios for you to consider. The first is dealing with the seller; the second is reading the broker. When the seller is represented by a broker, you must be prepared to do double duty. Whenever a middleman is involved, the negotiation process becomes more complicated. Another consideration is the type of property you plan to purchase. Different styles of property owners dictate the use of specific haggling skills. The seller of a small income property may react differently to your ideas than an elderly couple selling the home their children grew up in.

WHY IS THE SELLER SELLING?

The circumstances prompting the sale have a strong influence on your negotiating techniques. If the seller is on the doorstep of foreclosure, you are in a power position. When the seller is selling for convenience and profit, your position is weaker. It is important to find the reason for the sale before making an offer. There are many ways to formulate a hypothesis regarding the reason for a sale.

The most direct method is to ask the seller why the property is being sold. The answer you are given may or may not be true. To make the most of your buying power, you should investigate the circumstances surrounding the sale. If the property is worth making an offer for, it is worth looking into. A visit to the tax assessor's office is a good place to start your investigation. Property deeds are public information. You can inspect the seller's deed and examine it for clues.

Look for judgments, liens, or any other tangible evidence supporting a need for a quick sale. While you are there, look up the tax value of the property. The tax value is usually much lower than market value, but it will give you a basis for making an offer. In most cases, you will be able to see what the seller paid for the property when it was acquired. This type of information will be invaluable when formulating your negotiation strategy.

If the property's title is clouded with liens or attached by a judgment, you can assume the seller is anxious to sell. The outstanding attachments will also give you some idea of what the seller must realize from the sale of the property to satisfy the obligations. If you can buy the property below the assessed tax value, you should be on to a great deal. In most jurisdictions, tax value is well below market value. All this information is a matter of public record. There is no reason you should ignore the opportunity to take advantage of the opportunities afforded from learning such strategic information.

PEGGING THE PRICE PAID BY THE SELLER

If you can piece together the amount a seller paid for a property, you are in a better position to dicker. The transfer price (from when the seller purchased the property) should be a matter of public record. By checking the property transfers in the hall of public records, you should be able to determine exactly what the seller paid for the property. When the property is about to be lost, any profit for the seller is better than a foreclosure. The information gained from your diligent research will result in profitable rewards for you. While you are inspecting the deed, check for covenants and restrictions. These are two items you will want to know about; you might as well check them out while you examine the deed for other information.

PUTTING ON YOUR POKER FACE

Checking a property's deed is only one part of your job as a master negotiator. Your actions, beginning with the first showing of the property, will affect your bargaining power. To drive the best bargain, you must learn to control your facial expressions and comments. Experienced real estate brokers are adept at reading these signs. While you are looking at a house, the broker will be looking at you. The broker will also be listening to every comment you make. This is how a good broker finds your pressure points. When the broker has established your soft spots, she will move to force your hand.

With self-discipline, you can taint the broker's view of your opinions and emotions. This ability will give you a substantial edge in the negotiations for your real estate. When you learn to keep the broker and the seller guessing, you have much more control. If you telegraph your feelings through facial expressions, you will lose the bargaining battle. Maintaining a strong demeanor is necessary to effect an advantageous agreement for yourself.

CREATING AN IMAGE OF CONTROL

Exhibiting an air of confidence will have a positive effect on your purchasing power. When the seller sees that you are in control, he will have a higher regard for your offer. If you go about your property tour in an unorganized and hapless manner, the seller will assume he can beat you at the bargaining table. Knowing what you want and having a thorough knowledge of market conditions will play a big part in your confidence. Your written guidelines and checklists should make a lasting impression on the seller. Very few people are well organized and prepared when looking for a home. If it is obvious you are serious, the seller will take your offer more seriously.

PLAY IT CLOSE TO THE VEST

Be cautious in the comments you make while in the presence of the seller or his broker. Saying that you have looked at twenty houses and this one is the best you have seen will ruin your negotiation strength. Comments about how this home would be perfect for you are another no-no. Avoid giving any information to the seller that could be used as leverage in negotiations. If you are asked how soon you plan to buy a home, answer with a statement of control. Explain how you are prepared to buy a home today, but you want to find the best value and are willing to wait for the right house. Never say you have to buy a home within the next month because your lease is expiring.

LISTEN MORE THAN YOU TALK

In all negotiations, it is usually better to listen than to talk. Remember, from the day you begin your house hunting, your actions throughout the search will affect your negotiating power. Brokers are particularly perceptive and will notice most of your buying signs and weak points. Create an image of control from the beginning and never let the other guy know you are uncertain about your feelings. If you follow this rule, you will build a strong foundation for winning the price battle.

SETTING THE STAGE FOR A LOW OFFER

As you inspect the house, make notes on your checklists. Mumbling comments to your spouse may also help to build your case to offer a lower price. If you can find a crack in the drywall, point it out to your spouse. These hand motions will inform the seller you are aware of the home's deficiencies. This type of inspection will help you later when you must justify your reasons for offering a lower price for the property. The seller will remember your comments and checklists. This mental reminder will help persuade the seller to accept a lower price.

If you verbalize your comments, don't be insulting. You are in the seller's home and the wrong words may offend him. It is all right to point out defects, such as cracked drywall, but refrain from making negative comments about the seller's decorating tastes. If you think the purple carpet is ugly, relay your feelings tactfully. Don't tell the seller the carpet is horrendous and must be removed. Instead, comment on how the carpet will clash with your furniture and must be replaced with a different color. In both cases, you are bringing the cost of replacing the carpet to the seller's attention. In the first comment, you may offend the seller and lose any possibility of buying the house. The second method is much less derogatory and will not put you in bad standing with the seller.

TAKE THE HOUSE APART

The ability to make a strong showing of your own when touring properties will be very advantageous later. Look for any item in the home that may lower the property's value. Inspect countertops for burn marks. Check the insulation everywhere you have access to it. Essentially, take the house apart looking for flaws. Every defect you list can be used to drive the asking price lower. Make a point of bringing the defects to the attention of the seller and the broker.

BRINGING IN A PROFESSIONAL INSPECTOR

Before you have made a final commitment to purchase the house, you should have a professional inspection performed on the property. These can cost a few hundred dollars and are usually not done until a price has been agreed upon. The professional inspection is generally a contingency of your contract. If problems are discovered, you will be able to void the contract or negotiate for a lower price, if the contract is worded accordingly. While these professional inspections protect you, it will be your personal inspection that builds the case for a low offer.

Your initial offer will be made before the professional inspection. It would be silly to pay $250 for an inspection only to find the seller will not accept your offer. Instead of throwing your money away in this manner, make the professional inspection a contingency. Since the professional inspection will come after you have an agreed-upon price, you must use the results of your personal inspection to justify the price drop. This is a vital step in building your case for lowering the sale price.

Give Them the Facts

With so much riding on your ability to produce evidence suggesting a lower price, be thorough with your inspection notes. It is a good idea to submit a copy of your notes with the offer. This will show the seller you have a reason for offering less than he is asking for the home. If all you do is make an unsubstantiated low offer, the seller may refuse it without considering your reasons. By including a list of items requiring repair or replacement, the seller will at least understand your position.

ASSUMING THE ROLE OF APPRAISER

Once you have inspected the house, you will need to use appraisal techniques to determine a fair market value for the property. You don't need an elaborate education to accomplish your goal as an appraiser. While the results of your appraisal may not match the report from a licensed appraiser, you can get a good idea of what the house is worth. Your appraisal work will be on the elementary level and will not take all factors into consideration. You don't need to do a full-blown appraisal to establish your reasonable opinion of value.

Professional appraisers use many methods to establish a property's value. They evaluate the property in multiple formulas to average out a fair market value. You should not expect yourself to be capable of doing a first-class appraisal. For your purposes, working with the comparable-sale method will be adequate. This procedure is not too difficult, and the information you need can be obtained from varied sources. Remember, the following information will help you make a reasonable guess as to a property's value. It is not intended for use in producing an accurate appraisal. In the purchasing process, you will be paying a professional to appraise the property. This information is very condensed and should only be used to arrive at a ballpark figure.

An Abbreviated Lesson in Appraisal Techniques

The method of appraisal you will be using is known as the comparable-sale method. It is so named because it deals with comparing the property you wish to buy to other similar properties recently sold. To arrive at a true appraised value, this method is used in conjunction with other appraisal techniques. Since you are only interested in finding a starting point for negotiations, your opinion of value does not have to be completely accurate. Before you are firmly committed to buying a home, the home should be appraised by a licensed professional appraiser.

To establish a guesstimate of a property's value, the comparable-sale method will suffice. This is a rela-tively simple process: compare the house you are planning to buy to others that have sold recently. There is a form at the back of the chapter to help you: the Comparable Sales Comparison Sheet.

To complete this form, you will need detailed information about recent real estate transactions. If you are working with a real estate broker, she should be able to help. Most brokers belong to a Multiple Listing Service (MLS). These brokers receive books at regular intervals showing all real estate activity among the MLS members. They also receive books containing all the property sold over a period of time by the MLS members. These are known as comparable-sale books or comp books.

If your broker has access to these comp books, she can make your evaluation process easy. Look at the comp form in the back of the chapter. This is an example of the type of information contained in comp books. From these comp sheets, you can gather the information you need to establish an opinion of value. If you don't have access to comp books, you can research your project at the Hall of Records.

When properties are sold, their transfer is recorded among the public records. By checking these records and the tax assessment information, you can obtain the facts you need. This method is more time consuming than working with comp books, but it can still be accomplished in a few hours. Once you have compiled your information, you will compare the comparable sales to the property you are considering.

Since the columns on the Comparable Sales Comparison Sheet line up, it will be easy to look across the sheet for cost comparisons. Usually, you will have to make adjustments for the comparable sales being used. If you are using three comps, one of them may be much newer than the other properties. One of the comps may have four bedrooms while the others have three. These differences must be allowed for with cost adjustments. Try to locate comparable sales that were closed within the last six months. The comps with the most recent sale dates will work best.

When selecting your comps, try to make your selections as similar as possible. Look at the square footage of the home, the number of bedrooms, and other key items affecting a property's value. The closer your comps match the property under consideration, the more accurate your amateur appraisal will be. Professional appraisers have formulas and databases to work with when making cost adjustments. For your purposes, an educated guess with some substantiation will be fine. If you compare enough three-bedroom homes to four-bedroom homes, you will develop a feel for what the fourth bedroom is worth.

As you work through the comparison sheet, you will be establishing a basis for your offer to purchase. If you put together enough comparable sales, it will be apparent what the average value for these homes is. When you reach the bottom line, you should be able to decide what the subject property is worth to you. Your appraisal figure may be way off from the true appraised value, but you will have obtained a figure for what the home is worth *to you*.

DEFLATING INFLATED PRICES

By taking the time to complete a rough opinion of value, you will know much more about what the property you hope to buy is worth. Many homes are placed on the real estate market at inflated prices. This procedure is the result of wishful thinking by sellers and the influence of inexperienced brokers.

Many new brokers are not very experienced in appraisal techniques. Their lack of appraisal skills may result in an opinion of value lacking accuracy. Another reason brokers prompt sellers to list their homes at inflated prices is the hope of a larger commission. Most brokers are paid a percentage of the sale price. Obviously, the more a house sells for, the higher the commission to the broker. This mentality results in more stalled sales than large commissions. When a property is grossly overpriced, buyers will be reluctant even to make an offer to purchase. The broker would do much better to make a quick sale, at a realistic price, than to hold out for a huge commission.

PUTTING PRICES IN PERSPECTIVE

As time passes, the seller usually begins to lower the sale price. After a while, the broker will suggest lowering the price. If they had put the house on the market at a fair price to begin with, the home could have sold much sooner. When you begin to look at houses, you will notice wide discrepancies in asking prices. Your Comparable Sales Comparison Sheet will help to bring these house prices into perspective.

If a property is offered with an inflated price, your comp sheet can help to get your lower offer accepted. You will have proof that your offer is reasonable. By submitting your market research evidence with your offer, the seller will be forced to acknowledge the cold facts about the value of his property. Building a strong case with comparable sales is your most effective negotiating tool.

MAKING YOUR LIST AND CHECKING IT TWICE

Before going on your house hunt, you should make a list of your negotiation tools. To this point, you have a number of weapons in your arsenal. There will be more negotiating skills needed, but they will come after you are ready to make your offer. Your list should begin with an awareness of your emotions and comments. This is the first step towards winning the negotiations for your first home.

Image

Presenting an image of control should be the second item on your list. When you meet with the sellers or their broker, you will be presenting an image. It is critical that you present the proper image. Studying the market is the best way to develop confidence in your real estate knowledge. This knowledge will shine through and show the sellers that you are a serious buyer.

Finding the Right Property

The next step is to find a property you are interested in buying. When you do, establish why the seller is selling. The seller's motivation can play a big part in your purchase-offer strategy. Next, do some homework and find out what the seller paid for the property. This will give you some background information on what the seller may expect to get for the property.

The Inspection Strategy

If everything is still on track, go back through the house for a second tour. This second visit will have the seller and the broker excited. They will associate your second walk-through with a desire to purchase the home. This is where you employ the inspection strategy to build your case for a reduced price. Before going on this tour, be sure your guidelines and checklists are in order. Be prepared to exhibit your theatrical abilities to get your point across to the seller. Putting on a good show during the inspection will cement your interest, and also your disappointment, in the property. This will serve you well if you make a low offer.

Making an Opinion of Value

The next logical progression is to assemble information for your Comparable Sales Sheet. While you are doing this, the seller will wonder if you are going to buy the property. Your play in making the seller wait for your response should have a positive effect on your negotiations. When you have arrived at your opinion of value, you are ready to make your offer to purchase the property.

Up until now, you have been building the foundation on which to base your low offer. Now it is time to make the offer and to use your direct negotiation skills. When you enter this stage of the game, you will be dealing with the broker or the seller. In either case, a face-to-face negotiation is rare. Normally, you will submit a written offer and wait for a response. The following information will help prepare you for the progression of events to follow your offer.

MAKING THE OFFER TO PURCHASE

Chapter 12 reveals the technical mechanics of making your offer to purchase real estate. Here you will learn how to negotiate your offer. When you make

your offer, it should be a written offer. The offer should be accompanied by a package of documents supporting your reasons for the low offer. This might include your inspection results and comparable sales research. Include anything you feel will strengthen your case for a lower price. Whenever possible, avoid being available for questioning when making the offer. You don't want to be forced to make on-the-spot decisions. If your offer is submitted without your presence, the seller will weigh his decisions more carefully.

For example, if one of your contingencies is that the seller pays two points, he can't ask you whether you will accept the offer if he refuses to accept this contingency. If the seller alters your offer in any way, the offer is voidable by you. If you are not available for questioning, the seller may be afraid to strike out your contingency. He should know that if he deletes the contingency, you have the right to withdraw your offer. Distance in negotiations can be very beneficial.

Keep Your Distance

When negotiations are done at a distance, you do not have to make a snap decision. Having time to contemplate your next move will help you win the negotiation battle. If the seller is represented by a broker, avoid discussing the offer with the broker. Brokers are required to deliver all written offers to the seller. If you leave your offer in a sealed envelope at the broker's office, the broker will be unable to test you.

Brokers are professionals trained in sales tactics. Good brokers have the ability to manipulate people and to shift the leverage or "balance of power" in negotiations. If the broker wants to discuss the terms of your offer, keep your comments under control. Never show your hand to the broker. Don't answer "what-if" questions, and avoid discussing your offer beyond clarifying what the offer already says. A common strategy for brokers is to test you with "what-if" questions. The broker may ask you all types of questions to establish your flexibility in the terms of the offer.

The broker may hit you with an "If I could, would you?" approach. All of these phrases are professional sales terms. Don't answer any of these questions. Explain to the broker that you want your offer presented to the seller and will be waiting for the seller's response. Thank the broker for her time and excuse yourself. The less you say, the stronger your position in the negotiations.

THE SELLER'S COUNTER OFFER

If you are making a particularly low offer, the broker may try to talk you out of presenting the offer to the seller. She may tell you the offer will insult the seller. Sometimes this does happen with unfounded low offers. Since your offer will be backed up by evidence for the low offer, your risks of insulting the seller are reduced. If you feel your offer is reasonable, it won't matter if you insult the seller. You would not want to pay substantially more than your offered price, so if the seller doesn't want to play ball, you seek another house.

Some brokers will try to convince you they cannot present such a low offer to the seller. Nothing could be further from the truth. The broker is obligated to submit the offer and return the results of the offer to you. If you are asking a lot of the seller, you can expect a counter offer. The broker will probably want to present this counter offer to you in person. If you allow this meeting to take place, be careful. The broker will try to close the deal and will exert all her sales skills to do so.

When you meet with the broker, let her explain the terms of the counter offer. Don't comment on the terms unless you are certain that you have no further interest in the property. If the offer is ridiculous, feel free to reject it on the spot. If there is still hope of striking a deal, don't make any comments about the counter offer. The broker will ask you how the counter offer looks and will try to read your expres-sions. Tell her that you are willing to think about the counter offer and ask her to leave it with you.

YOUR COUNTER OFFER

Get the broker out of the way and study the counter offer. If the standing counter offer is acceptable, you can accept it and return it to the broker. If you feel the property is worth pursuing but not at the standing terms, decide what your counter offer to the seller will be. Follow the same procedure you did with the first offer and get your counter back to the seller.

This back-and-forth trading of paperwork may go on for days. The key element in winning the game is *making your case* to justify the price drop. If you invest the time to compile supporting evidence, the seller should view your position as valid. If he doesn't, look for another house. There will always be stubborn sellers who will not consider your proposed price drop. These sellers are impossible to work with and are easily identified. Your first counter offer will tell you if the seller is willing to be reasonable.

SUMMING IT ALL UP

Of all the advice given, building a comprehensive package to justify your actions is the single most important factor. If you show the seller a list of other houses currently for sale and how they closed, he should understand the justification in your offer. Pointing out the number of days his property has been for sale can have a sobering effect. Many sellers never realize they have been trying to sell for 120 days until you remind them. A detailed list of defects found on your inspection builds credibility to justify your low offer. All this evidence will soften the seller's price if he is rational. In the long run, following this advice will cost you time, but it should save you money.

COMPARABLE SALES COMPARISON SHEET

SUBJECT	COMP 1	COMP 2	COMP 3
Square Footage	_____	_____	_____
Lot Size	_____	_____	_____
Utilities	_____	_____	_____
Number of Rooms	_____	_____	_____
Number of Bathrooms	_____	_____	_____
Number of Bedrooms	_____	_____	_____
Kitchen	_____	_____	_____
Family Room	_____	_____	_____
Living Room	_____	_____	_____
Den	_____	_____	_____
Laundry Room	_____	_____	_____
Basement	_____	_____	_____
Attic	_____	_____	_____
Storage	_____	_____	_____
Construction	_____	_____	_____
Interior Condition	_____	_____	_____
Exterior Condition	_____	_____	_____
Parking	_____	_____	_____
Schools	_____	_____	_____
Location	_____	_____	_____
Price	_____	_____	_____

COMMENTS

11

What You Must Know About Financing

There are not only many types of loans, there are numerous variations of the same kinds of loans. To get you started, I am going to show you each of the most common types of loans and discuss their variations and important features. After all the loans have been identified, I will show you how to see what type of loans you might qualify for. I will also show you common formulas and ratios used to determine the maximum amount you may borrow.

LOAN RATIOS

The complex part of establishing how much home you can afford comes from your own evaluation. Commonly, a commercial lender approves you for a loan that may make you miserable in the future. When a loan officer projects your borrowing power, he works with standard loan ratios. These ratios may not take into consideration factors that are of the utmost importance to you. Different types of loans have various qualifying ratios, but most conventional loans have two standards.

Most loan officers use either 25/33 ratios or 28/36 ratios. To use these ratios effectively, a loan officer will look at many factors. The first key element is your *gross income*. The loan officer will take your gross income and multiply it by either 25% or 28%. The choice between the two ratios will be determined by how conservative the lender is. For this example, assume the lender will use the 28% ratio. Assume your gross annual income is $35,000. The loan officer will determine that 28% of your gross

income is $9,800. He will then divide this number by twelve to determine how much you can afford in a monthly payment.

The amount arrived at will be $816.67. This is the first step in determining what the bank will allow you to have in a monthly mortgage payment. The second step is a little more complicated. In the second step, the loan officer will find what 38% of your gross annual income is. The amount is then divided by twelve to give you a monthly figure of $1,108.33. This amount represents the maximum amount of your monthly mortgage payment and long-term debts. Long-term debts include, but are not limited to, credit cards, car payments, and installment loans. Depending on the type of loan you want, the definition of long-term debt may change. Some lenders don't count loans with fewer than six monthly payments left. Other lenders may not hold loans with fewer than twelve remaining monthly payments against you. Credit cards will almost always be considered a long-term debt.

From the $1,108.33 figure, you must subtract the total monthly payments for all your long-term debt. The remaining number represents your maximum borrowing power. Assume you have a car payment of $200 and credit cards with monthly payments of $85. This is a long-term debt of $285 per month. When you subtract $285 from $1,108.33, you are left with $823.33. The loan officer will compare this with the first number he obtained when computing 28% of your income. That number was $816.67.

When you compare $816.67 to $823.33, the loan officer will give you a preliminary approval for a monthly house payment, including taxes and insurance, of $816.67.

According to the lender, you can afford to pay $816.67 for your monthly housing expense. This number was chosen because it was the lower of the two ratio results. You must be qualified with both types of ratios and accept the lower of the two amounts as your maximum monthly payment. You can use these same ratios to get an idea of how much loan a lender will approve you for. There is a form at the back of this chapter to help you estimate your lender-based borrowing power—the Lender-Based Qualification Worksheet. Refer to the above example if necessary to complete the form.

Once this worksheet is complete, you will have a very good idea of how much the bank will allow your monthly payment to be. The monthly payment must include the cost of real estate taxes and hazard insurance. Don't forget to place an estimated amount for these figures on your worksheet. If you omit these items, your projected loan amount will be way out of line.

CONVERTING THE MONTHLY PAYMENT TO A LOAN AMOUNT

With your projected monthly payment established, you may want to convert it to a loan amount. Refer to the Estimated Mortgage Loan Calculation Table at the back of this chapter to make the conversion. The directions for converting the net monthly payment into a loan amount are detailed in the table. When this conversion is complete, you will know approximately how much money the average lender will loan you. The next piece of your affordability puzzle is the expense of your closing costs and points.

Closing Costs and Points

For this phase of your experiment, assume closing costs and points amount to about 5% of your loan amount. There will be times when they may not exceed 3%, and at other times, they may exceed 5%.

If you allow 5% of the loan amount as an estimate, your figures will be pretty accurate. Take the loan amount from your monthly payment conversion and multiply it by 5%. This is the amount of cash you are likely to need in addition to your down payment. The amount of money required for a down payment is your next consideration.

DOWN PAYMENT

Down payment amounts fluctuate with different types of loans. For a qualified veteran of the military, there may not be a down payment required. For most people, a minimum down payment will be 5% of the sale price. As financing requirements tighten, 10% down payments are becoming more common. When you identify the amount of down payment required, you will have all the elements of your lender-based affordability index. The next section will summarize your needs, to establish how much home a lender may say you can afford.

EXAMPLE OF A LENDER-BASED AFFORDABILITY CONCLUSION

You have determined how much the lender will allow you to allot for a monthly mortgage payment. This monthly payment has been converted to a loan amount. Using an estimate of closing costs and points based on a percentage of the loan amount, you know how much money you need for these fees. By judging your loan amount, closing costs, points, and down payment requirements, you have determined the maximum amount you can spend for a new home. This is all based on an average financial institution's opinion of your repayment capabilities.

With this figure established, you should have some idea of whether the amount seems reasonable to you. In many cases, you may say that there is no way you can afford such a house payment. If that is the case, your work is just beginning. Your instincts on what you are comfortable in paying for a monthly house payment should be acknowledged. Lender ratios are not an exact science. There are many considerations that sterile ratios ignore. Do you enjoy an expensive vacation each year? Do you engage in an expensive hobby? Do you like to eat at expensive restaurants on the weekends? These factors will not be considered in a lender's standard ratios. Give it a lot of thought. If you are uneasy, there is probably a good reason.

VETERANS ADMINISTRATION LOANS

To be eligible for Veterans Administration loans, one of the borrowers must have a certificate of eligibility from the government. If you or your spouse have been in the military, Veterans Administration (VA) loans offer many advantages. With this type of loan, the seller is required to pay points for the acquisition of the loan. With the seller paying these points, your closing costs will be much lower. This means you will not need as much cash to buy your first home.

A big advantage to VA loans is the fact that you are not required to make a down payment. The combination of reduced closing costs and no down payment allows you to buy your home with very little cash. For first-time buyers, accumulated cash savings are one of the biggest stumbling blocks to get past. A VA loan will enable you to offset your lack of savings. Interest rates for VA loans are competitive, and the rate is fixed for up to thirty years.

Sellers may be resistant to accepting an offer to purchase with VA financing involved. They may not be willing to pay the points. The seller could have other negative feelings about a VA loan. VA loans are reputed to be slow in processing and very demanding of a property's condition. They are strict on the physical characteristics of a home, but this aspect provides additional protection for you. An inspector must approve the property before a VA loan will be granted. The time to process the loan is slightly longer than a conventional loan. Horror stories told about waiting six months to close a VA loan are a result of incompetent people involved in the loan processing.

These less-than-competent people could be real estate brokers, loan originators, or loan processors. The paperwork involved in a VA loan is extensive and must be completed correctly. If the people submitting the loan to the VA are negligent, the paperwork will be rejected. This is where the slow processing time comes from; it is not the VA's fault. The problem rests in the private sector. When the VA loan requirements are compiled and submitted accurately, the loan will close promptly.

The combination of increased paperwork, property inspections, and seller-paid points contributes to a negative attitude to VA loans. You must not allow these factors to deter you if you are qualified for a VA loan. It may take a while to find the right people to work with, but when you do, the results will make your efforts worthwhile.

The qualifying ratios for a VA loan are very liberal. VA loans may be obtained to purchase residential properties with single-family homes and multi-family buildings with up to four apartments. The veteran must certify his intention to occupy the property as a primary residence.

Spouses of military personnel killed or missing in action (KIA or MIA) may be eligible for VA loans. For a veteran entitled to full benefits, the VA will guarantee a loan without a down payment, for a prescribed amount. The local lender can have the loan guaranteed by the VA for up to the maximum allowable amount. If the veteran wishes to purchase a home above the maximum guarantee, he may do so by providing a cash down payment. The veteran must meet the requirements of the lender to be certified creditworthy before the loan is guaranteed.

While the loan ratios for a VA loan are very liberal, they are also very complicated. A rule-of-thumb qualifying ratio is that 41% of the gross income may be used for a house payment, real-estate taxes, and long-term debt.

Expenses such as utility bills, life insurance, and food are not factored as long-term debts. The VA loan has many conditions and factors affecting an individual's qualification. Consult a knowledgeable broker or loan officer to determine the precise loan amount you will qualify for. As an example: if your combined household gross income is $40,000 per year, you would be allowed to spend $1,366.68 for your combined long-term expenses and housing expense per month.

To determine how much you can spend on your home, tally up your long-term debts and credit card debts. Subtract the total of the monthly payments from the $1,366.68. If your car payment is $250, your student loan is $100, and your credit card payments are $80, your total long-term debt is $430. When you subtract $430 from $1,366.68, you are left with $936.68 for your house payment, hazard insurance, and property taxes. If the property taxes for the house you wish to buy are $75 per month, subtract $75 from $936.68. You are left with $861.68 to spend each month on your new home and insurance. If the insurance premium is $25 per month, you have $836.68 for your house payment.

To convert this monthly amount into a house price, refer to the Estimated Mortgage Loan Calculation Table at the back of the chapter. Assume an interest rate of 9% for a term of thirty years. Find the 9% rate on the amortization chart, and look across the chart at the amount in the thirty year column. The figure in the column is $8.05. This represents what you will have to pay monthly for every $1,000 borrowed. Now, divide your monthly allowance of $836.68 by the $8.05 factor. You will come up with a number of 103.94. This number represents how many thousand dollar increments you may finance. Multiply 103.94 by 1,000, and you will see you may finance a maximum of $103,940.

When you are formally qualified by your loan officer, there may be some difference in the amount you are actually qualified to borrow. The VA qualifications take many factors into consideration when establishing your qualifications. For the average person, understanding all the factors is difficult and unnecessary. Using the 41% example, you will get a very good idea of your qualifications. A real estate broker or loan officer who is familiar with VA financing can determine your exact qualification. Either of these professionals should be willing to qualify you without charging a fee.

FEDERAL HOUSING AUTHORITY LOANS

Federal Housing Authority (FHA) loans are an excellent choice for the first-time buyer without VA eligibility. FHA loans allow you to finance some of your closing costs, and the down payment requirement is less than that of most loans. Qualifying ratios for FHA loans are lenient; there are no special requirements for a person to be eligible for an FHA loan.

The Federal Housing Authority is a division of the U.S. Department of Housing and Urban Development (HUD). FHA does not make loans; it insures loans made by approved lenders. FHA loans are available with fixed interest rates and for terms up to thirty years. The maximum loan amount for an FHA loan varies with geographical locations, depending upon the cost of local housing. The maximum loan amounts are fair and more than adequate for most first-time buyers.

You may purchase a single-family home or up to a four-unit apartment building with FHA financing. Unlike a VA loan, the recipients of an FHA loan do not have to occupy the property. If FHA financing is being used to purchase investment property, a substantial down payment is required. For the owner-occupant, down payment requirements are minimal. You must have a down payment equal to 3% of the first $25,000 borrowed and a 5% down payment for all monies borrowed in excess of $25,000.

There are some exceptions to this down payment requirement. Owner-occupied single-family residences with a maximum appraised value of $50,000, including closing costs, require only a 3% down payment. If the property you are buying is less than one year old and not built to conform with FHA regulations, a 10% down payment is required. The amount of closing costs you may finance varies from location to location.

Most FHA loans require a mortgage insurance premium (MIP). This premium is collected at the time of closing and may be financed in the loan for the property. If the MIP is paid in full at closing, it may be paid by someone other than the purchaser. It could, under these conditions, be paid by the seller or a parent.

FHA will recognize sweat equity as all or part of your down payment. There are specific guidelines to be followed, but you may use your labor in lieu of down payment. This opportunity exists with a home being built or renovated. Properties being financed with an FHA loan at the minimum down payment must first be inspected and approved by an authorized inspector. To see how much you qualify for with an FHA loan, review the following example.

Qualification criteria for an FHA loan are difficult for the inexperienced person to comprehend. Instead of giving you all the contingencies of FHA qualifications, I will give you a rule-of-thumb qualifying procedure. With most loans, including FHA loans, you must use two different formulas to establish your borrowing power. When you have calculated both formulas, the one with the lower allowable monthly payment is the one that determines your qualifications.

The first qualifying number is found in this manner: multiply your annual gross household income by 28%. Then, divide the resulting number by twelve. The number arrived at will be the amount of money you are allowed for house payment, taxes, and hazard insurance. As an example: your income is $40,000 per year. Multiplying $40,000 by 28% will give you $11,200. Then divide $11,200 by twelve to arrive at your maximum monthly payment: $933.33. This is the first step in qualifying yourself.

The second step requires your gross annual income to be multiplied by 36%. In doing so, you arrive at a figure of $14,400. Divide that number by twelve to get $1,200. The $1,200 figure is the maximum amount you are allowed for house, taxes, insurance, and long-term debt. Assume you have a car payment of $250. Your monthly credit card bills are $50, and you have an installment loan with a monthly payment of $60. Your monthly long-term debt is $360. You must subtract the $360 from the $1,200 figure. This will give you the maximum amount you may spend for house, taxes, and insurance — $840.

Now, compare the first monthly allowance you determined with the second one. In the first qualifying test, you were allowed $933.33 for your house payment obligations. In the second test, you were allowed $840. You must abide by the lower of the two numbers; in this case, you may spend $840 per month for your house and related expenses.

Using the amortization chart, as you did with the VA loan example, you may borrow up to $104,348. To determine your down payment requirement, follow this example. To keep it simple, assume you are buying a $100,000 home. Let's also assume you have enough money to pay for closing costs without financing them. For the first $25,000 borrowed, you will need a down payment of $750. The remaining $75,000 will require a 5% down payment, equal to $3,750. This makes a total down payment of $4,500.

QUALIFYING FOR A CONVENTIONAL LOAN

To qualify yourself for a conventional loan, use formulas similar to those used in the FHA example. Liberal lenders will use the same 28% and 36% factors to qualify you. Conservative lenders will substitute ratios of 25% and 33% for their qualifying guidelines. The monthly-payment qualification procedure is the same as shown in the FHA example.

There can be big differences in the down payments required for conventional loans. Some conventional loans require a 5% down payment; others require a minimum down payment of 10%. The down payment is established by the lender and is sometimes related to the type of conventional loan applied for. The down payment percentage is based on the total sale price as stipulated in your contract to purchase the real estate.

Credit requirements are often more strict with a conventional loan than with an FHA loan. If your credit rating borders on being poor, you will have more trouble obtaining a conventional loan. Interest rates for conventional loans are competitive and sometimes even lower than VA or FHA loans. Your closing costs may not be financed with conventional financing, but the seller can usually pay a percentage of the cost for you.

Conventional loans are available in numerous configurations. There are pros and cons to each type of loan. In the following descriptions, you will learn about many of the most common conventional loans. Loan programs change quickly, so it will benefit you to talk with a loan officer before making plans based on a certain style of loan.

CONVENTIONAL LOANS

Thirty-Year Fixed-Rate Loan

The thirty-year fixed-rate loan is the most easily understood conventional loan. It allows the borrower to repay the principal and interest over a period of thirty years. The interest rate never changes during the thirty-year term. These loans are considered by many to be the standard real estate loan.

Typical down payments for an owner-occupied loan of this type range from 5% to 20% of the purchase price. With very good credit, a 5% down payment is adequate for many lenders. Some lenders have recently increased the down payment requirement to 10%. With less than a 20% down payment, private mortgage insurance is required for the loan. This insurance adds additional cost to the monthly payment. Private mortgage insurance companies are very strict on credit requirements. If your credit is less than good, expect your down payment requirement to be at least 10%.

The big advantage to the fixed-rate loan is knowing what the monthly payment will be for the life of the loan. You are assured that your payment will not increase over time. The disadvantage to the loan is the interest rate. Since the rate is never increased, it usually starts at a higher percentage rate than for other conventional loans. While the thirty-year fixed-rate loan has been an industry standard, it has lost much of its appeal. Alternative conventional financing methods now overshadow the old workhorse loan.

Adjustable-Rate Mortgages

Adjustable-rate mortgages (ARMs) built a bad reputation for themselves when first introduced. People flocked to them for low interest rates, but were unpleasantly surprised later. Some of the original ARMs utilized negative amortization. With negative amortization, you could pay on the loan for years and still owe more than you originally borrowed. This problem made it impossible for many people to sell their homes. Negative amortization is no longer a part of the average adjustable-rate mortgage.

Another problem with early ARMs was the unlimited interest rate increases possible. The first ARMs were not limited in the amount the interest rate could escalate. They were not equipped with annual or lifetime caps. These ARMs did not offer a conversion feature to allow the borrower to lock in a certain interest rate. In general, the borrower had no control over and no idea of how much his house payment would be from one year to the next. All this has been corrected with current adjustable-rate mortgages.

Adjustable-rate mortgages allow the interest rate to fluctuate with the economy. In modern loans, this fluctuation is limited by "caps." There is an annual cap and a lifetime cap on most new ARMs. A typical ARM might have an annual increase cap of 2%, with a lifetime cap of 6%. These caps protect the borrower from runaway interest rates. The interest rate cannot go up more than 2% in any given year. The rate will never exceed 6% of the original interest rate. These caps provide protection, but the best ARMs are coupled with a conversion feature.

The conversion feature allows the borrower to lock into the interest rate some time after originating the loan. Normally, this action may be taken after the first or second anniversary of the loan origination. This gives you the option of making the ARM a fixed-rate loan for the remainder of the loan's term. A fee is usually charged to convert the loan, and conversion fees vary greatly. They can be as little as a few hundred dollars but may be considerably more. Let me give you an example of how these loans work.

Assume that a thirty-year fixed-rate loan is available with an interest rate of 11%. The adjustable-rate loan is available with a starting rate of 7%. The

ARM is equipped with a 2% annual cap and a 6% lifetime cap. It also has a conversion feature, with a conversion fee of $500. The conversion may be done anytime after the second year of payments. The down payment and qualifying requirements are identical for both loans. Which is the better loan?

If you take the fixed-rate loan, you are paying 11% interest for thirty years. If you choose the adjustable-rate loan, you start off with an interest rate of 7%. Assuming the worst, the ARM interest rate will go up 2% each of the first two years. At the end of the second year, it will cost you $500 to convert to a fixed-rate loan. Starting with an 7% loan, increasing the rate 2% each year will result in a rate of 11% when you do your conversion. This is the same rate the fixed-rate loan started with. The adjustable-rate loan is the better choice in this example.

During the first year of payments on a $100,000 loan, the fixed-rate payments would be $11,427.88. The fixed-rate loan would have similar payment requirements in the second year, for a total of approximately $22,855.76. The first year payments on the ARM would be $7,983.60. The second year payments would be about $9,655.44, for a total of $17,639.04. Adding the conversion factor of $500 to the ARM payments would bring the total to $18,139.04. The adjustable-rate loan cost approximately $4,716.72 less than the fixed-rate loan. For the remaining twenty-eight years, both loans will demand the same payments. This example shows the power of shopping for a good adjustable-rate loan.

ARM Indexes

How do ARMs work? Interest rates for adjustable-rate mortgages can go up or come down. If you have an ARM and the economy is good, your payment could decrease by the same amounts possible for an increase. ARMs are tied to an index. The type of index varies, but could include Treasury Bill Rates, Treasury Note Rates, Federal Reserve Discount Rates, or the Cost of Funds Index. These are all published indexes, readily available for consumer inspection.

Shopping for an Adjustable-Rate Mortgage

Shopping for a good adjustable-rate loan requires paying attention to detail. Beware of extremely low entry-level rates. These "teaser rates" are often well below the agreed-upon contract rate for the loan. In less than a year, your payment could increase dramatically. Confirm that the starting interest rate is equal to the contract rate of the loan before accepting the mortgage terms.

Ask the lender what the adjustment interval for the loan is. This figure reveals how often your interest rate may be changed. The adjustment interval could be set on a monthly basis, an annual basis, or any other time in between. Try to find a loan with an adjustment interval set on an annual basis. When discussing the adjustment interval, inquire about the types of caps used on the loan.

There are two types of caps, an interest cap and a payment cap. Insist on a loan with an interest cap. With an interest cap, you know what parameters your interest rate may move in. Payment caps only ensure the increase limits on your monthly payment. They do not limit the increase of the interest rate. With only payment caps, you could fall victim to negative amortization. While your payment remains at a certain level, the interest rate could go on unchecked. If you are faced with this type of loan, run in the other direction. Negative amortization is a very dangerous financing tool to use. After years of payments, you could owe more than you borrowed.

Growing-Equity Mortgages

Growing-equity mortgages (GEMs) are a worthwhile consideration for buyers expecting increased incomes in future years. With a GEM loan, the payment will increase at predetermined times to reduce the principal amount of the loan. These increases are frequently 5% or less and are set for a specific period of time. The increased amount is applied directly to the principal, reducing the loan amount quickly.

Growing-equity mortgages are based on a thirty-year amortization schedule. If you anticipate increased earnings on an annual basis, a GEM loan could save you substantial money in interest charges. Your interest fees will be less, and the loan will be paid off much sooner with a growing-equity mortgage.

Graduated-Payment Mortgage

Graduated-payment mortgages (GPMs) are exactly what they sound like. They are loans starting with low monthly payments, with increasing payment amounts as the loan matures. Negative amortization plays a part in the GPM loan. If you need a break on monthly payments to buy your first home, these loans could be the answer. The drawback is the increasing payment and negative amortization. If you only plan to own the home for a few years, these loans could be worth looking into. When you are trying to finance a home with long-term plans for residency, avoid the GPMs.

OTHER OPTIONS

The types of financing available are extensive, but the ones mentioned above are the most common. There are many other types of creative financing available, but for most people, the ones discussed earlier in this chapter are the most viable options. When you venture into more exotic types of creative financing, you need a polished professional to explain their intricacies. Some of the less common financing plans are listed below.

Graduated-Payment Adjustable-Rate Mortgages (GPARMs) are a blend of a GPM and an ARM. *Pledged-Account Mortgages* (PAMs) utilize a cash reserve deposited as collateral in an interest-bearing account. These loans are sometimes known as *flexible-loan insurance programs* (FLIPs). *Shared-appreciation mortgages* (SAMs) were very popular for a time, but they are no longer common. They involve an investor participating in the ownership of the property with the resident. The investor benefits from tax advantages, and the homeowner benefits from a minimal down payment. Both investor and owner share in the increased equity of the property for a predetermined time. Then the property must be refinanced or sold to buy out the investor.

There are still other highly-specialized loan programs that have not been discussed. These loans are so rare that they are not worth the average home buyer's consideration. You certainly should be able to find some loan among those profiled to suit your needs. Knowing what you can afford is the first step you must make as a potential homeowner. With all this loan information, you are well prepared to ask key questions of your broker or loan officer.

Armed with this information, you should be able to project a reasonable range of homes that you are qualified to buy. Consult with a loan officer before getting into deep water. Every lender may have a different rule for qualifying you. At present, the given ratios are accurate, but lending requirements can change abruptly. Use this as a starting point, but talk with a knowledgeable professional before committing yourself to a transaction.

LENDER-BASED QUALIFICATION WORKSHEET

25%-33% RATIOS

Gross Monthly Income _____ (A)

25% of Gross Monthly Income _____ (B)

The amount in "B" represents the first number in the qualification procedure.

Gross Monthly Income _____ (C)

33% of Gross Monthly Income_____ (D)

Total Monthly Expense for Long-term Debt _____ (E)

Subtracting "E" from "D" will give you the second number needed in the qualification procedure. Compare the numbers resulting from the two different procedures. The lower number is the amount you will qualify for in a house payment. Remember, this amount must include real estate taxes, principal, interest, and hazard insurance. To use the 28%-36% ratios, simply make the adjustments in the percentages used in the calculations.

ESTIMATED MORTGAGE LOAN CALCULATION TABLE

To obtain a payment amount, multiply the amount in the table by the amount of the loan in thousands. EXAMPLE: If the interest rate of your proposed loan is 10%, find 10% in the Interest Rate % column. Read across into the column with 15 or 30 year terms. Use the multiplier in these columns to determine the approximate monthly payment. With a 10% rate, a $100,000 loan amount, and a 30 year term, multiply $100,000 X 8.78 to arrive at a monthly payment of $878.

INTEREST RATE %	15 YEARS (per $1,000)	30 YEARS (per $1,000)
7	$8.99	$6.66
7.25	9.13	6.83
7.50	9.28	7.00
7.75	9.42	7.17
8	9.56	7.34
8.25	9.71	7.52
8.50	9.85	7.69
8.75	10	7.87
9	10.15	8.05
9.25	10.30	8.23
9.50	10.45	8.41
9.75	10.60	8.60
10	10.75	8.78
10.25	10.90	8.96
10.50	11.06	9.15
10.75	11.21	9.34
11	11.37	9.53
11.25	11.52	9.71
11.50	11.69	9.90
11.75	11.84	10.09
12	12.01	10.29
12.25	12.16	10.48
12.50	12.33	10.67
12.75	12.49	10.87
13	12.66	11.06
13.25	12.82	11.26
13.50	12.99	11.45
13.75	13.15	11.65
14	13.32	11.85

12

Making the Commitment and Offer to Purchase

When you have found the perfect property, you must make the commitment to submit a purchase offer. Until the time comes to make the commitment, you feel sure of yourself and your wish to buy your first home. When it is time to make the big commitment, you may feel less certain. The thought of making a long-term, high-dollar commitment can scare anyone, especially a first-time buyer.

THE BUYER'S BLUES

No matter how much you prepare yourself, the final commitment will seem ominous. At first, it may be overshadowed with excitement, but within twenty-four hours, the reality of your actions will settle in. When this happens, you may be terrified, confused, and excited all at the same time. This is a natural reaction and is to be expected. It is also natural for you to second-guess your decision and consider backing away from the deal. This is called "buyer's remorse."

Unless you are unique, you can count on at least a touch of the buyer's blues. When these feelings hit you, deal with them and put them away. If you do your homework first, there will be no reason to second guess your buying decision. If you have any doubts, settle them before you reach the stage of making an offer. Once the offer is accepted, you are committed to the deal. This is no time to change your mind.

PUTTING YOUR FEARS TO REST

You Know What You Can Afford

What questions must be answered to put your commitment fears to rest? The most common fear is centered around the buyer's ability to pay for the home. If you follow the guidelines in Chapter 1, you know how much house you can comfortably afford. By projecting your monthly budget, you know approximately what you are willing to spend on a house payment. When you compare the house payment to your rent payment, there may not be much difference. This is especially true if the tax advantages of home ownership are considered.

If You Move, You Lose; Or Do You?

If you can buy your own home for about what you are paying in rent, why shouldn't you make the commitment? There is only one viable reason for deciding *not* to invest in a home under these conditions. Buying a home does restrict your ability to relocate quickly and easily. In most cases, you would have to sell your home before you could move. When you are renting, it is generally much easier to move on short notice.

In some occupations and locations, this factor might be worth considering. Buying a home in a town with little employment opportunity could be a hardship if you lose your job. When you are likely to be transferred, putting down roots may be a mistake.

This is a consideration that you must take into account on a personal basis. Look at your circumstances and decide whether buying is a good idea.

If relocation or employment opportunities are not a problem, there should be no reason for not buying a home. You have to live somewhere, whether you are paying rent or making mortgage payments. Owning your own home offers many personal and financial benefits. Make this decision before making an offer to purchase a home.

The Needs and Desires Question

Chapter 2 taught you to distinguish between needs and desires. If you followed those instructions, you know what your minimum housing requirements are. You are also aware of the features you would like the home to have. If the house you are about to make an offer on fits the criteria, there is no reason for idle speculation to slow you down.

Building Toward a Decision

In Chapter 3, you explored the pros and cons of building a new home compared to buying an existing one. Climbing the stairs to commitment one step at a time makes the decision to buy easy. If you make each commitment as you come to it, the final commitment will be made with confidence. When you are unsure of your decision, the fear factor will consume you. Address each issue and make firm decisions as you progress to the offer stage.

Handyman Hang-Ups

The lure of handyman specials was covered in Chapter 4. By now, you should know if you are interested in building sweat equity through fixer-uppers. Go through Chapter 4 again if you feel it necessary to make a decision on a handyman special. Don't move on to another phase until you have this question answered. Handyman specials are known for causing confusion among real estate buyers. Remove this confusion from your mind before making any commitments.

Broker Intervention

Chapter 5 examined the value of working with real estate brokers. This has little to do with your deci-

sion to make a final commitment, but a broker can have a strong influence on your buying decision. Don't overlook the advice given on brokers. If you understand how brokers work, you will be less vulnerable to second thoughts on your buying decision.

Inspection Fears

In Chapter 6, you were instructed in the key elements to look for in your first home. It concentrated on the importance of a thorough inspection of the property before making an irreversible decision. If you follow these instructions, there will be little reason to doubt your assessment of a property. With professional inspections, you can rest easy with your decision to buy the home.

You Know Where to Look

Chapters 7 and 8 schooled you in methods of finding special opportunities. When you are able to find a desirable property at an unusual price, there won't be much need to question your decision to purchase the property. All of these decisions are important in deciding to purchase your home. Taken in small pieces, they are easy to handle. If you wait until the last minute to address them, they can overwhelm you. Establishing a comfort level is easier once you are organized.

Building Confidence

In Chapter 9, you were exposed to the risks of letting your emotions cloud your logic. In addition, the chapter gave you tips on defining your buying criteria. Buyer's remorse is an emotion. To control this powerful emotion, all you have to do is be comfortable with your decision. Following the right steps will raise your confidence in the commitment you have made to purchase a home.

Play All Your Cards

In Chapter 10, you learned how to make your best deal. Reviewing this information should make you feel better about your decision to move ahead with the purchase offer. Applying the techniques in Chapter 10 will help you negotiate wisely and get your best price for the house. If you use these techniques, don't sit around wondering if you could have gotten the home for a lower price. Play all your negotiation cards before making the ultimate commitment.

The Financing is Available

Chapter 11 educated you in real estate financing. With all those options, you shouldn't have any trouble finding a financing plan that will satisfy you. When you determine what type of financing suits your needs, specify it in the offer as a contingency. This will assure you the right to obtain your desired financing or to void the contract. You may wonder if your loan will be approved, but you will not have to wonder if you made the right decision on the financing.

Professional Help

The professional help you will require is discussed in Chapter 14. With the list of professionals and your preliminary interviews, you will know where you stand. The support of these professionals will relieve you of the stress of making all the decisions on your own. Since they are professionals, you should put faith in their advice. If you have any doubts, get a second opinion. Ultimately, you must trust and depend on the advice of professionals.

FACE YOUR FEARS FIRST

This chapter deals with commitment and the proper preparation of your offer. You stand out on the edge of one of the largest financial commitments you have ever faced. Fear and confusion can cause many problems at this point. If these feelings exist, you will miss out on much of the excitement you should experience in buying your own home. These ugly emotions can taint your judgment and force you to make a bad decision. There is no room for fear or confusion in your mind when making such an important decision. I know that this paragraph may have elevated your stress level, but you must face these fears before making any offers.

If you are convinced you are making the right move, then do it! If there are any doubts, work them out now. If you are afraid or confused, define the cause for the unwanted sentiments. Don't try to look at the entire picture and extract the pieces bothering you. Take each fear and deal with it on a one-to-one basis. One of the easiest ways to accomplish this is by making a list of your concerns.

Organize a list with your concerns on it. Take your time and list every item you are worried about. When the list is complete, evaluate the concerns. Pinpoint the cause of your uncertainty. If you are not comfortable with how to structure your offer, talk with your broker or attorney. If the fear is financing, meet with your loan officer and review your financing plan. Whatever the problem, address it and get it solved before making an offer to purchase your house.

CALL YOUR LAWYER

When you arrive at a decision, it is time to make an offer. With all your fears set aside, you will be able to put together a winning proposal for the seller. Eliminating your confusion will open your mind, so you can concentrate on the elements of your offer. At this stage, you should consult with your attorney. If you are working with a buyer's broker, the broker can put the offer together for you, but an attorney is your best choice. Be sure the attorney is familiar with real estate deals. Not all lawyers are adept in real estate law and principles. You want an attorney who specializes in real estate transactions.

Your attorney will advise you on the fine points of real estate law. It will be up to you to tell the lawyer what you want in the offer beyond standard legal jargon. This is where you must put your thinking cap on. The potential for contingency clauses may well be endless. It would be foolish to fill the offer with unneeded clauses, but leaving out the wrong clause could be unsettling.

To be able to communicate with your attorney, you must have some idea of what clauses pertain to you. What follows is an explanation of common contingency clauses. Review them and note the ones that may be applicable to your offer. When your list of possible contingencies is complete, review them with your lawyer. This is the safest way for you to proceed with the purchase of your property.

CONTINGENCIES

In each of the following contingencies, you are requesting the right to approve the results of the contingencies. You are reserving the right to cancel your contract subject to the outcome of the contingencies. With the proper wording, your contract will be voidable, without penalty or loss of your deposit, if the contingencies are not removed to satisfaction.

Any language entered into your purchase offer should be prepared or reviewed by your attorney prior to submission to the seller. The contingency clauses shown throughout this chapter are only examples. Consult with your attorney to determine the proper wording for your purchase offer.

Financing Contingency

The first contingency to be discussed is found in the majority of all real estate purchase offers. It is a financing contingency. This clause details the type of financing you wish to obtain and the financing terms you will accept. Normally, if the prescribed financing is not available, you may void the contract. The clause might look like this:

> Purchaser will apply for financing within five business days of the acceptance of this offer. Purchaser will finance 90% of the sale price for thirty years with a fixed-rate loan, with amortized monthly payments. The interest rate for the loan shall not exceed 10.75%. The purchaser will have the option of prepaying the loan without penalty. Purchaser will pay up to, but not more than, two discount or origination points. If purchaser is unable to obtain a loan meeting these terms, the purchaser shall have the right to void this contract and have the earnest-money deposit returned within three days. Purchaser will seek financing from at least three commercial lenders before the contract becomes voidable. If financing is not available to the purchaser, purchaser shall not be penalized for the inability to obtain financing.

Inspection Contingency

Another common contingency allows the purchaser to have various inspections performed before being committed to complete the real estate transaction. Some of the items the clause may pertain to are:

- Air radon
- Water radon
- Structural conditions
- Mechanical systems
- Environmental scans
- Insect infestation
- Septic systems
- Water quality
- Water quantity
- Roof condition
- Code violations
- Asbestos

These are only some of the inspections that could be covered with an inspection contingency clause. Any item you feel should be investigated could be included.

Title-Search Contingency

A title-search contingency assures you of receiving a good and marketable title to the property. The contingency will allow you to have a title search performed before closing on the house. If the title is found to be clouded or defective, you will have the right to void the contract if the seller cannot correct the title defect in a reasonable time. This is a standard contingency found in most real estate contracts.

Survey Contingency

A survey contingency provides you with the opportunity to have the property surveyed before closing. This contingency is common when the seller does not have a recent certified survey. The clause assures you of receiving all the real estate the seller has promised you. The survey can also disclose zoning violations, code violations, and properties located in hazardous zones.

If the property has been added onto over the years, the addition may be in violation of local ordinances. Erecting an addition too close to the property line would serve as an example of this risk. If you purchased the property without a survey, you would assume the addition was legal and on your property. It may turn out the addition violates setback requirements and must be removed. This is a very costly situation you want to avoid.

Your prospective new home may appear to be in a normal location while in fact it may be in a flood zone. Full-scale mortgage surveys will indicate any problems you may have with your new home's location. Properties situated in flood zones or flood plains are very expensive to insure. Quality surveys can protect you in many ways. In addition to these advantages, they will also identify easements and rights-of-way that may affect your ownership of the property. Survey clauses will be written along the same lines as all other contingency clauses. Your broker or attorney can help you with the insertion of these clauses into your purchase offer.

Soils-Test Contingency

When you are buying a parcel of land to build your house on, you may need a soils-test contingency. If the building lot is not served by a municipal sewer, you will have to install a septic system. Before a septic system can be installed, a suitable site must be found on the property. Depending on location, these tests may be performed by county employees or a private engineering firm.

Buying a building lot that will not meet perk-test requirements will result in your inability to build your home on the property. To meet perk-test requirements, the soil must be of a type satisfactory for septic systems. This requires having the soil examined and approved for a septic permit. Many sellers have these tests conducted prior to placing the property on the market, but the test is not required to sell land. If you assume the land is suitable for a septic system, you could be in for a bad surprise. When buying rural land, insist on a satisfactory soils-test contingency.

The soils test contingency might be worded this way:

> Purchaser shall at his expense have a soils test conducted to prove suitability of the property for a residential dwelling. The septic design must be for a normal system capable of supporting a four-bedroom home. If the land requires an unusually expensive system, the purchaser may void this contract without penalty or loss of deposit. If the property will not support a suitable septic system, the purchaser will not be penalized in any way for terminating this contract. Purchaser's earnest-money deposit will be returned within three days if this contract is voided due to an unsatisfactory soils test.

Covenants and Restrictions Contingency

This contingency protects you from purchasing a property with limitations on the use or alteration of the property. Some areas restrict many aspects of home ownership. To protect yourself from unknown restrictions, use a covenants and restrictions contingency clause.

A sample clause might read:

> This contract is subject to the purchaser receiving and approving any and all covenants and restrictions pertaining to this property. Purchaser may void this contract, without penalty, within three days of receiving copies of the covenants and restrictions.

These are only a few of the many possible contingency clauses to include in your purchase offer. Your attorney or broker will advise you of specific clauses pertinent to your offer. Any language entered into your purchase offer should be prepared or reviewed by your attorney prior to submission to the seller. The contingency clauses shown throughout this chapter are only examples. Consult with your attorney to determine the proper wording for your purchase offer.

PREPARING A WINNING OFFER TO PURCHASE REAL ESTATE

In most transactions, the sellers will make their decisions based on the written offer they are presented with. The way your offer is structured can have a strong effect on the seller. If the offer is sloppy and vague, the seller will probably reject it. When the offer is filled with hooks and traps, the seller will definitely reject it. A well-prepared offer will impress the seller and reveal your ability to purchase the property.

From your point of view, you want to slant the offer to favor your position. The seller will want the offer to provide the most benefits to him. There is an art to making the offer appeal to the seller, while protecting you. Contingency clauses are your best form of protection. It is important for you to include all contingency clauses that may affect your purchase of the property. It is equally important not to fill the offer with unreasonable or unneeded clauses. The cleaner you keep the offer, the better your chances are the seller will accept it.

INCLUDE TIME-FRAMES FOR PERFORMANCE

Including time-frames to remove contingencies will make the seller more comfortable. The seller will not want to tie up his property for an indefinite period, only to have you void the contract. When you request a contingency, place a time for its removal in the offer. For example, if you are inserting a contingency for a water-quality test, set a specific date for your removal of the contingency. The wording might look like this:

This type of contingency clause serves the best interests of the purchaser and the seller. As the purchaser, you are protected from buying a house with polluted water. The seller is assured his property will not be tied up by the contingency for more than ten days. Following this sort of guideline with all of your contingencies will make them more acceptable to the seller.

ELEMENTS OF A WINNING PURCHASE OFFER

Deposits

The earnest-money deposit has a lot to do with the way a seller interprets your offer. Most brokers will attempt to have you make a large deposit with your offer. The broker has two motivations for this request. First, if the offer is accompanied by a large deposit, the seller will assume you have the financial ability to obtain a loan. Second, if you default on the contract, the seller and the broker will have a large deposit to retain as liquidated damages.

I have made $250,000 real estate deals with a $100 deposit. There is no legal reason you should give a large deposit. In most states, a promise for a promise is all that is required to make a contract binding. Money is not an essential element of a legal contract in any state that I know of. If you wish to show your financial strength but don't want to put your money up until the offer is accepted, you can do a two-stage deposit. Submit a modest deposit with the offer and guarantee to increase the deposit by a set amount when it is accepted. This gives the same show of strength without putting your money in limbo while the offer is being negotiated.

Who Holds the Money?

When detailing information on your deposit, dictate the escrow agent. Will the broker hold the money?

This contract is subject to the purchaser, at his expense, obtaining a satisfactory water test from the property's potable water supply. The test will be conducted by an independent laboratory within ten days from the date this offer is accepted. At the end of ten days, the purchaser will remove this contingency from the contract with a written contingency release or may void the contract if the water-test results are unsatisfactory. If the purchaser voids the contract, he will not be penalized in any way and his earnest-money deposit will be returned within three days.

Will the seller's attorney hold the deposit? Will you earn interest on your deposit while it is in escrow? Think about suitable terms for the disposition of your deposit and have your attorney word the offer accordingly.

Timetables

Providing timetables for your performance will make your offer more attractive. Set a reasonable time for making loan application and removing contingencies. When the seller knows what to expect, he will be less leery of accepting your offer. Open-ended, vague offers are not conducive to making a good impression on sellers. Allow yourself adequate time for the tasks at hand, but include a date for your actions to be completed.

Property Descriptions

For your own protection, specify the legal description of the property being purchased in your offer. A street address should be used for the common description of the home, but the legal description is a vital element of your offer. Legal descriptions usually consist of a lot, block, and section number. These descriptions are obtained from the deed of the property. The deed will be available for your inspection at the Registry of Deeds. I know of two cases in the last ten years when people nearly bought the wrong property by using only street addresses.

In older properties, the legal description will be in the metes and bounds format. The description of the property in the deed is the one that should be used. Your attorney will know how to obtain the proper legal description if you ask him to include it in your offer. By using the description in the deed, you are assured of receiving title to the intended property.

Chattel

Chattel is personal property. It may include appliances, window treatments, wood stoves, and related personal property. In real estate, one might assume chattel is a part of the real property. If you look at a house and see that it has a range, a refrigerator, and a wood stove, you might assume they are included in the sale price. These items are personal property and are *not* necessarily included in the price of the house.

To avoid confusion and hard feelings, describe any possible personal property on which you are basing your offer. If your offer is made with the assumption that appliances will be included, state clearly in the offer your intention for the appliances to convey. This is an area in which many buyers are unaware of the proper procedure for ensuring that chattel is included in the sale price. Your broker or attorney can help you to identify other types of chattel. In general, if the item is not permanently attached to the real estate, it may be considered personal property. Good advice is to include a list of all items about which you have any doubts.

Ask for a General-Warranty Deed

The type of deed you are willing to accept will be another common element of your purchase offer. The best type of deed to request is a general-warranty deed. There are other types of marketable deeds, but some are not as good as others. Quitclaim deeds can be a problem. Quitclaim deeds offer very little protection to the purchaser for potential deed disputes. Talk with your attorney to obtain a full disclosure on the types of deeds available in your state.

Picking a Price

The price you are willing to pay is obviously a key element of your offer. This element is simple enough; you know how much you are willing to pay, and that is the amount you include in the offer. If you feel you need help in this area, consult with your broker or review Chapter 10 for negotiation tactics.

Contingencies

List all the contingency clauses you feel pertain to your offer. Review the earlier section of this chapter for details on contingency clauses. Don't include clauses you don't need. Keep the body of the offer clean and attractive to the seller. Remember to provide appropriate time-frames for removal of your contingencies.

Pro-Rated Fees

Pro-rated fees are an area of the offer you should pay attention to. In most cases, established annual expenses, such as property taxes, will be prorated to the day of closing. Inspect your pro-rating clause to determine how other items will be treated. If the oil tank is full, is it included in the sale price or will you have to pay extra for the oil at closing? In the case of income property, will the rents be pro-rated at closing? What happens with security deposits the seller is holding? You should receive the security deposits so they can be returned to the tenants at the appropriate time. The pro-rating clause is often skimmed over, but it should be scrutinized for your protection.

Who Bears the Burden?

Who is responsible for insuring the property while it is under contract? Normally, it is the seller's responsibility to maintain insurance until you take title to the property. This is the normal procedure, but there is nothing to say the contract could not require you to maintain insurance. This is an issue worth checking out. Try to arrange for the seller to accept responsibility for the property until the transaction is completed.

Wear and Tear

There should be a clause requiring the seller to transfer the property to you in a condition equal to the condition at the time it was placed under contract. You must allow for reasonable wear and tear, but protect yourself from negligent abuse. If the property is substantially abused, the value at closing could be much less than it was at the time you agreed upon a sale price. This is a common clause that no seller should object to.

When Can You Move In?

Normally, the purchaser takes possession of a property when the title is transferred. This is not guaranteed if the contract is worded to provide otherwise. Clearly define the date upon which you will take possession of the property. In most instances, this date will be the same as your closing date.

For more precise advice, consult with an experienced real estate attorney. Laws vary from state to state, and some of this information may not apply to you. Lawyers may not be cheap, but they are an excellent value when you are dealing in real estate. The money you could lose far outweighs the expense of a good attorney.

Listen to the brokers, but take their advice with caution. Brokers should be knowledgeable of real estate law, but they are not attorneys. Some brokers will be more interested in making a quick commission than in looking out for your future. I like to think these greedy brokers are few and far between, but they are out there. It is up to you to be responsible for your actions. Even real estate professionals need other professionals from time to time. As a new home buyer, you owe it to yourself to consult competent professionals.

This book will help you identify trouble spots. It will also make you aware of questions to ask the professionals. It will *not* replace local real estate professionals. Read the book, broaden your knowledge, and seek professional help before submitting a purchase offer. This preparation will protect you from making a serious and long-lasting mistake.

13

What to Expect When Your Offer Is Accepted

The events leading up to making an offer to purchase real estate are many. All the elements must come together at the right time and place to make you want to buy a particular home. When everything works out, you will submit your offer to purchase a home. Once the offer is on its way to the seller, you will be flooded with emotions. Your mind will dance with anticipation while you impatiently wait for the seller's response to your offer.

During this waiting period, you will be consumed with excitement. If the seller accepts your offer, you will be well on your way to owning your own home. You should feel a certain satisfaction from the effort you have exerted to make your dream a reality. Many buyers believe once their offer is accepted, it is a downhill race to home ownership. Getting the property under contract is a major step towards becoming a homeowner, but there is still much to do.

When your offer is returned and becomes a contract, the work is just beginning. This is when you must switch your emphasis from finding the right house to upholding your end of the deal. The seller has agreed to your terms. Now it is up to you to perform the duties expected of you in the contract. To ensure a timely closing, you will also have to supervise and coordinate the work of many people.

The events following acceptance of your offer are critical to getting your first home. If you assume the deal is done when it is signed, *you are wrong*. More things kill real estate deals during the last few weeks before closing than at any other time. If you don't pay attention to detail all the way through the closing, you can lose your opportunity to become a property owner.

As any experienced broker will tell you, the most vulnerable period in your acquisition is the time between loan application and closing. This chapter is dedicated to informing you of the procedures to be followed once you have a signed contract. When you first receive the signed contract, celebrate! Take enough time to enjoy the moment and work through your elation. When you have your feet back on the ground, prepare to get serious. This is the time you must be alert and responsive to fast-changing conditions. You will be required to fill many shoes and make many more important decisions.

GOOD ORGANIZATIONAL SKILLS HELP

With strong organizational skills, getting to a successful closing will be much simpler. During this time, you must mix patience with an aggressive demeanor. Your faith and mental strength may be tested from time to time. The path from contract to closing can be rocky and tenuous. Learning to distinguish when you should accept circumstances and when you should strive to change them will be challenging. The following advice will prepare you for the obstacles you may have to overcome.

REMOVING CONTINGENCIES

When your purchase offer becomes a contract, you must get busy. The first order of business is to satisfy any contingencies in the contract. Normally, you will have an agreed-upon time limit to remove the contingencies or void the contract. Don't procrastinate on this phase of your work. If you exceed the time limit, you may lose the deal or be forced into purchasing the property. Dated contingencies are only a safety net while they are active. Once the date for performance passes, the seller is in control.

Start removing the contingencies with the least cost involved to settle. Starting with the least expensive contingencies can save you money. If the early, inexpensive contingencies kill the deal, there is no reason to pursue the more expensive ones. Organize all your contingencies and satisfy them in order of priority and cost. When you get to the financing contingency, refer to the tips and procedures detailed in Chapter 11.

FINANCING

Chapter 11 advises you on how to approach various lenders for a loan. When you are prepared, make a formal loan application. The information in Chapter 11 explains enough about various loans to give you an idea of what to talk with your loan officer about. When you have made a formal loan application, your work with the lender is not complete.

In a few days, you will receive a truth-in-lending statement from your financial institution. This form terrifies many first-time buyers. It shows you the annual percentage rate (APR) of your loan and the total cost of your home, including finance charges. The APR is usually higher than the interest rate your payment is based on. This little detail confuses almost all new buyers. The total amount of principal and interest payments is enough to force you to faint. Be prepared for this shocking statement and don't let it get the better of you.

When you pay discount points to the lender, it is reflected in the APR. These points can be looked upon as prepaid interest. The result is an APR higher than the interest rate your payment is based on. The total money spent to finance the house will be shocking. When you consider paying 10% interest on your mortgage for thirty years, the total amount becomes very large. This mammoth sum can cause you to have second thoughts. While the amount of money paid is huge, it is an investment. You are obtaining many advantages from becoming a homeowner, and few people can pay cash for their home.

Locking in Your Interest Rate and Points

When you make formal loan application, you will have to decide whether you want to lock in your rate and points. This decision will require you to gamble. If you lock these items in, you must accept them when the loan is closed. Locking in a 10.5% rate at loan application can make you sick if the rate is only 9% when the loan is ready to close. You will be obligated to pay the 10.5% rate even if the current market rate is 9%. The same concept applies to the discount points. Points can go up or down on a daily basis.

If you decide not to lock in the rate and points, you could regret it at closing. There is no guarantee these items will not escalate in the coming weeks. By locking them in, you know what to expect at closing. If you decide to let the rate and points float, you have no idea what they will be when you have to close the loan. There is no advice to give you on this subject that can be relied on. You will have to monitor the market and make your best guess.

Most people prefer to lock in the rates and points. They may have to pay more, but at least they know what is required of them. Your broker or loan officer can help you decide on the best course of action regarding interest rates and points. The decision is a personal one. Careful attention to the market and studying historical data can also help with your decision.

Preliminary Loan Approval

The day you obtain preliminary loan approval is one you will remember for a very long time. After formal loan application, you will have to wait, sometimes for weeks, to see if your loan will be approved. Waiting can be the hardest part of buying your first home. You want to see action, but the wheels of financial institutions can turn very slowly. The loan processing procedure may need to be pushed along from time to time.

With most mortgage companies, the person who helped you apply for the loan will not be the individual processing your loan. Once the loan is applied for, you will need to deal with the loan processor. This person is responsible for sending out employment verifications, credit requests, and other required documents. If this process is slow, and it usually is, your tentative loan approval will be held up.

Staying on Top of the Loan Processing Procedure

If you are working with a broker, the broker should stay on top of the loan processing procedure. If you are going it alone, the responsibility is yours. Someone must keep tabs on the loan processor. Processors are hounded constantly by impatient brokers and buyers. To obtain the best results, the processor must be handled diplomatically. If you or your broker are a pest, your application may get misplaced in the reams of paper on the processor's desk. If you don't prod the processor, the customers screaming the loudest might get serviced before you do. There is a delicate line between being too aggressive and being too passive. Be pleasant but persistent.

Time Your Calls

About ten days after loan application, check in with the processor. Inquire to see if your paperwork is in order and if you can be of any assistance. Don't become pushy or arrogant. You want the processor to expedite your application. The wrong approach can cost you weeks of time in the loan approval process. Call the processor each week for a status report. These professionals expect you to be anxious and will generally be helpful and supportive, if you approach them with polite respect.

Under normal circumstances, you may receive preliminary approval in less than a week. If the lender must send your verifications out of state, the process could take several weeks. During this time, you

must combine patience with persistence. Keep in touch with the processor, but don't call every day. When the preliminary approval is issued, you are cruising towards home ownership.

SWEATING OUT THE APPRAISAL PROCESS

After the lender issues preliminary loan approval, an appraisal will be needed. The appraisal will be performed by an appraiser approved by the financial institution. Appraisals can wreak havoc with an otherwise easy deal. If the property does not appraise for enough, you will have a serious problem.

When a low appraisal is reported, you and the seller must make some decisions. The bank will base the loan amount on the appraised value or the contract amount, whichever is lower. Their loan-to-value ratio will be computed on the official appraisal. When this amount is lower than expected, most contracts are voidable. There should be a contingency in the contract to deal with a low appraised value. In most of these clauses, you have the option to void the contract or renegotiate the terms of the contract.

You could ask the seller to lower the sale price to the appraised value. If he will do this, you don't have a problem. If he won't, the ball is in your court. You could put more of your money into the deal to offset the low appraisal. There are two problems with this approach. First, you are paying more than appraised value for the property. Except for rare circumstances, this is not a good business move. Second, you will need more cash to apply to your down payment. If a compromise cannot be met, the contract will have to be terminated.

Expect Appraisal Problems

Appraisal problems are common and should be expected and taken account of in the back of your mind. If you have a good broker, the broker may be able to influence the appraisal. The broker may be able to dig deeper to find credible comparable sales. If the appraiser can be shown evidence to support increasing the appraised value, he will. I know of many occasions when the first appraisal was a deal-buster. With some work on my part, I was able to achieve a higher value.

To justify a modification in the estimated value, you will need verifiable facts. You or your broker will have to give the appraiser different comps to work with. If the appraiser is not accustomed to working in your location, he may not be privy to some private sales. Many appraisers obtain their sale comps from the local multiple listing service. The MLS only reports activity conducted by its members.

Dig for Gold

If you are willing to scour the local Hall of Records for private sales, you may strike gold. It is possible to turn up private transactions to overturn the first appraisal. If your evidence is conclusive, you have a good chance of winning your case. During your journey from contract to closing, never take anything for granted. There will be pitfalls along the way, any one of which is capable of thwarting your closing.

THE LETTER OF COMMITMENT

Shortly after preliminary approval, you will receive a letter of commitment. This letter guarantees your approval for a loan to purchase a home. The letter will specify all the terms and conditions of your loan approval. When this letter comes, you will be asked to sign the letter to accept the described financing terms.

Before signing the commitment letter, read it thoroughly. There could be an inadvertent mistake in the terms or conditions. The letter could describe terms and conditions different from your expectations. Don't just sign and return the letter. Have your attorney inspect the letter for any questionable language. Once the attorney approves the letter, you should sign and return it to the lender. After this is done, you can breathe easier. With your written loan commitment, proceed with the chores required to take title to the property.

THE TITLE SEARCH

Once your loan is approved, your lawyer will begin title search proceedings. This process could reveal problems with the title. If the attorney finds the title to be clouded or unmarketable, you will not wish to settle on the property. The likelihood of severe title problems is remote. If defects are found, they will probably be easily corrected by the seller. Title searches are usually not a time-consuming process for an experienced real estate attorney.

If the title is clouded, the seller will be advised of the problems and asked to correct them. In the event these defects are not removed, it would be unwise to close on the property. Typical title defects include mechanic's liens, judgments, and disputed ownership. In the case of liens and judgments, they can often be removed with money. If the seller wants to sell the house, he can ask the closing agent to pay the debts from his proceeds at closing. Normally, this is all you will encounter with most property transfers.

If the ownership of the property is disputed, your closing will be more difficult. Someone must resolve the dispute and clear the title for a proper transfer. This process can get expensive and be very time-consuming. These occasions are rare, but they exist. Most transactions are not unduly affected by defective titles. This concern should be low on your priority list of items to worry about. Your attorney will take care of these details and will not allow you to settle on the property until the title is acceptable.

INSURANCE

When you are given a date for your closing, you must arrange for hazard insurance (homeowner's insurance). Insurance policies are normally paid for prior to closing. The insurance agency will provide you with a binder to prove insurance has been issued for the property being purchased. Evidence of insurance will be needed at the closing table.

Most lenders will require the insurance to name them as the first insured. This guarantees the lender that their interest in the property is protected. They will only require insurance in an amount equal to the loan amount. For your protection, the policy should be for an amount equal to the appraised value of the home. It is common for a hazard policy to include your personal possessions. When you get to this point, shop for your insurance coverage. Prices and policy features vary. You should check with several companies to ensure that you are getting your best deal.

GETTING YOUR EARNEST-MONEY DEPOSIT TO THE SETTLEMENT

I have been to closings at which the escrow agent failed to deliver the earnest-money deposit. The escrow agent knew the deposit was needed but neglected to bring it. This mistake can cause the closing to stall and may require the whole procedure to be postponed. To ensure a simple closing, talk with the escrow agent before the settlement date. Confirm that he will have your deposit at the closing table.

WRITER'S CRAMP

The closing process takes from thirty minutes to two hours. The type of loan you chose will dictate the amount of paperwork required to close the loan. Government loans involve extensive paperwork, but all loans require several signatures. At the closing, your broker and your attorney should be present. You will be asked to sign countless forms and agreements. Most of these documents will contain hundreds of words and may take substantial time to read.

Many buyers sign the documents without reading them. While this is a common practice, it is not a good one. When you sign these papers, you are committed to fulfill their terms. It may seem embarrassing to take the time to read each word, but it is your right and you should exercise it. If you don't understand what you are reading, consult with your attorney.

After all the papers are signed and the money changes hands, you own the property. This will be your first day as a full-fledged homeowner. After the documents are all executed, your attorney will need to record them. Recording the documents is very important. If the documents are not recorded, you could be at risk. For your ownership to be acknowledged, the documents must be properly recorded in the Registry of Deeds.

BONUS INFORMATION

The preceding information outlines the basics of closing your loan. Throughout this endeavor, there are some other points worthy of your attention. The requirements of a successful closing are sometimes extensive and complicated. For a novice buyer, the process can be intimidating and confusing. The remainder of this chapter will zero in on some additional details pertinent to a triumphant settlement.

The closing process is not complicated, but it can cause stress levels to rise when incompetent people are encountered. As a buyer, your loan is of the utmost importance to you. To the people processing the loan, it may just be another day at the office. This single fact is enough to frustrate the average home buyer. Now that you know the principles involved with closing your loan, let's investigate various people who can cause the event to be uncomfortable.

THE LOAN ORIGINATOR

Your loan originator is the first of many professionals you pass by in reaching the end of your settlement journey. If you have been pre-qualified for the loan, taking this step should be simple. You present your loan package, pay the loan application fees, and sign the necessary forms. During this time, the loan originator is all smiles. Many loan originators are paid a commission for every loan they originate. Your loan application may very well result in a personal financial gain for the loan officer.

If you are working with a broker, she will usually accompany you on the formal loan application. With preliminary planning, formal loan application is no big deal. You will need your loan package and your checkbook. From this point, the challenges can become much more trying.

THE LOAN PROCESSOR

After making formal loan application, you will be assigned a loan processor. If you get an experienced processor, you might not encounter any problems. This hope is not likely to prove true. Loan processors are typically the first of many elements to raise your blood pressure. Much of the processor's job will depend on the type of loan you have applied for. If you applied for a VA loan, expect some problems.

Veterans Administration loans require extensive paperwork. (All government loans involve more paperwork than the average conventional loan.) Anytime you increase the demand for paperwork, you increase the odds for a mistake. If your processor is not familiar with the procedure for processing a VA loan, your application could be rejected. If this happens, it is usually due to insufficient information from the processor. There is no problem with your qualifications; the problem lies in the paperwork. This type of rejection does not kill your loan, but it does slow the whole procedure.

You are somewhat helpless once formal loan application is made. You cannot force the other people involved to do their job efficiently. If your loan is not being processed in a timely manner, exert friendly pressure on the processor. If your loan is being neglected completely, talk with the supervisor for the mortgage department. If you have a good broker, she will take care of this for you. Brokers don't get paid until the transaction is closed, so they have an interest in expediting your loan approval.

THE APPRAISER

The appraiser is a very important player in your real estate game. With a low appraisal, you have big problems. In most cases, the lender will choose the appraiser to estimate the market value of your anticipated new home. Most lenders will allow you to choose the appraiser if you are applying for a conventional loan. The financial institution will expect the appraiser you select to be on their approved list. If your appraiser works full-time in the area, the chances are good he is on the lender's list.

If you are applying for a government loan, you will not be able to pick your appraiser. Appraisers for these loans are selected at random, on a rotating basis. This procedure ensures a fair appraisal without any outside influence. Since neither you nor the lender can pick the appraiser, the appraisal results will be unbiased.

Most appraisal reports will support the sale price of a home, but there can be problems. If the property is overpriced, the appraisal will disclose this fact. You or your broker may have to work with the appraiser to make the numbers work. If the first appraisal comes in low, you can request another appraisal or work to raise the value of the first one. This procedure was discussed earlier in the chapter.

INSPECTIONS

Removing your contingencies will frequently involve the use of professional property inspectors. To expedite your loan proceedings, prepare a list of the professionals you may need in advance. When the time comes to act, you will be able to move quickly. If you wait until the last minute, you may find that none of the inspectors is available. If this is the case, your lack of planning will slow down the transaction. This is an area of the closing process you can control. With a list of professionals and scheduled dates, you can be on top of your job.

SETTING UP YOUR INSURANCE

When you know your loan is approved, make arrangements for hazard insurance. You will need this coverage in place before the lender will close the loan. Apply for the insurance at least a week before closing. While you are waiting for loan approval, you can shop insurance rates. Make the best use of your time and don't drag your feet on tasks that must be done. There are many things beyond your control; don't allow *yourself* to be one of them. Instigate all areas of preparation at the earliest feasible date.

THE ACTUAL CLOSING

When you get to the closing table, you may be confused by the proceedings and overwhelmed by the paperwork. To avoid this problem, have a mock closing with your attorney beforehand. Ask your lawyer to go over the procedure and to explain the forms you will be asked to sign. To see where your money is going, you will be given a closing statement. (See the Estimate of Seller's Proceeds and Estimate of Purchaser's Closing Costs at the end of the chapter.) In this way, your attorney can prepare you for the closing in advance. This advance preparation will save time and confusion on the big day.

FINAL WORDS

Don't assume you are out of the woods when your offer is accepted. Until the loan is closed and the transaction is recorded, anything can happen. During the interim between loan application and closing, stay involved and keep busy. It is not unreasonable for you to request periodic updates on your closing status. When working your way to closing, be diplomatic. If you are overly aggressive or offensive, your closing can be set back for weeks.

You may walk a thin line between being persistent and being a pest. If you are working with a broker, request weekly updates on the events leading to the closing. If you are on your own, test the waters and stay involved. If you perceive a resentment for your regular requests on your closing status, back off. There is no way to give you a guaranteed set of rules to follow. You have to use your own judgment to establish how much pressure is too much.

The important thing to remember is, if you don't follow up on the events affecting your closing, you may not see a successful closing. Be willing to provide additional information when it is requested. Cooperate with the professionals working your deal and let them do their job. Normally, a weekly update is all that is required to keep your closing on schedule. If you are unsure of what to do, consult with your broker or attorney.

ESTIMATE OF SELLER'S PROCEEDS

Sales price (A) _____

Amount of first mortgage _____

Amount of second mortgage _____

Amount of other liens _____

Total of loans and liens (B) _____

Gross equity (subtract B from A) (C) _____

Estimated Costs:

Escrow fees _____

Document preparation fees _____

Broker commission _____

Legal fees _____

Prepayment penalty _____

Transfer tax _____

Pest control fees _____

Repairs _____

Recording fees _____

Discount points _____

Origination points _____

Trustee fees _____

Notary fees _____

Prorated taxes _____

Interest _____

Loan payments in arrears _____

Prorated rents _____

Security deposits _____

Prepaid rents _____

Other: _____

Other: _____

Total costs (D) _____

Credits:

Prorated prepaid taxes _____

Other credits: _____

Other credits: _____

Other credits: _____

Total credits (E) _____

Estimated net cash proceeds (C minus D plus E) _____

ESTIMATE OF PURCHASER'S CLOSING COSTS

Sales price   (A) _____

Estimated Costs:

Escrow fees _____

Document preparation fees _____

Loan origination fee _____

Legal fees _____

Loan assumption fee _____

Transfer tax _____

Pest control fee _____

Loan application fee _____

Recording fees _____

Points _____

Trustee's fees _____

Notary fees _____

Prorated taxes _____

Interest _____

FHA/MIP (mortgage insurance) _____

Inspection fees _____

Credit report fee _____

Hazard insurance _____

Title insurance _____

Down payment _____

Other fees _____

Total costs   (B) _____

Credits _____

Credits _____

Credits _____

Total credits   (C) _____

Estimated total cash need for closing = (B) minus (C) _____

Total estimated closing costs $ _____

14
Attorneys, Accountants, and Other Professionals

When you buy your first home, you will deal with numerous professionals. To make your home-buying efforts more productive, you should know who these professionals are and what they do. The people involved in your purchase can have many effects on your real estate acquisition. The turning point in deciding if the outcome of their efforts will be good or bad can rest on your shoulders.

The best professionals can make mistakes if they are working with incomplete or inaccurate information. During your home purchase, you will supply a good deal of information to the experts involved. If you give them poor information, they may not be able to do their jobs properly. This failure can result in delays or even the destruction of your deal. Since you will be required to depend on professional service, you should know what to expect. This chapter will inform you of the many people you may work with to buy your home. You might not work face to face with these people. In fact, many of them you may never talk to directly. Some specialists work behind the scenes.

Buying a home is a big decision, and it can account for stress on your part. Between the stress and the seemingly endless waiting, your nerves can become frayed. If you understand how much work is involved with your home purchase, it may make it easier to accept the waiting. By knowing *who is doing what*, at least you will understand *why* the process can take so long.

Some of the authorities noted below will not be involved in your purchase. There are many factors determining who is needed to reach a successful closing. The type of financing has a lot of bearing on the number of people involved. The physical condition of the property and the location can alter the collection of professionals needed. What follows is a description of the most common professionals encountered when buying a home. Since real estate brokers were profiled in Chapter 5, they are not highlighted here.

YOUR ACCOUNTANT

When you talk with brokers about buying your first home, they will play up the advantages of home ownership for tax purposes. There are generally tax advantages involved with owning your own home. To determine what tax benefits you may take advantage of, you should consult a Certified Public Accountant (CPA).

Real estate brokers are limited in the tax information they may provide. For you to explore all your tax options, you need a tax expert. In a one-hour consultation, you can get a strong overview of the advantages buying a home will offer you from the tax angle. This tax information can make a big difference in your comfort level on a house payment.

Most new buyers compare their present rent payment with their proposed house payment. They assume if they can only afford $600 per month for rent, that is all they can afford in a mortgage payment. In many cases, this is a false impression. Study the following example to see how the tax benefits may help you to afford your first home. Keep in mind: *this is only an example*. Each individual will be affected differently by the tax advantages of home ownership.

Tax Advantage Example for Home Ownership

Assume you are renting an apartment with a monthly rent of $600. This is the most you feel comfortable with for a monthly housing expense. You have VA eligibility and can buy a home without a down payment. Your concern is the monthly payment on your new home. You know there will be hazard insurance and real estate taxes to pay on a home. How will all this affect the style and price of home you can buy?

For this example, assume that your hazard insurance will be $25 per month. Your real estate taxes are $75 per month. With these two factors known, you believe you can afford $500 per month for your house payment. If the interest rate for VA loans is 10%, how much house can you afford under this plan? By financing the home for thirty years, you can afford a home loan of about $56,975. Depending upon where you are, this may not buy much of a home.

Now consider the possible tax advantages. As a homeowner, you may be able to deduct much of your mortgage payment from your income taxes. For this example, assume that your combined income is around $40,000 per year. Also assume you can deduct your mortgage loan interest and taxes. Since the bulk of your house payment is interest, assume a monthly deduction of about $535. Your personal situation may dictate different figures, but follow this example to understand the tax savings involved in homeownership.

With a $535 monthly deduction, you may see a tax benefit of $150 or more. If this holds true, your net house payment is only $450, not $600. Since you are comfortable with a rent payment of $600, how

much house will a net payment of $600 buy you? Using the same terms and rates as above, you could borrow about $74,068. In this example, the tax savings allow you to spend an additional $17,000 and still realize the same net payment.

With this type of impact, tax advantages are well worth examining. The cost of a one-hour consultation will be small change compared to your potential gain. Please remember: this example is *only* an example. Before you count your tax refund dollars, talk with a CPA. In most situations, there are many tax advantages to look at. Your tax professional will be happy to explain all of your tax advantages and consequences.

THE SELLER'S ATTORNEY

The seller's attorney is one professional with whom you may have very little contact. This lawyer works for the seller, but you should have some idea of what the attorney will be doing. The seller's attorney provides many services for the seller. This attorney does not work for you, but her actions may affect you. This attorney may be responsible for advising the seller on how to deal with you. She may request specialized information on the transaction to protect her client.

With this in mind, you should try to maintain a pleasant relationship with the seller's attorney. She will most likely represent the seller at closing. The seller's attorney will be in communication with the brokers and with your attorney. She may be the escrow agent for the seller. All her efforts will be for the benefit of the seller. Talk with your attorney for a full understanding of this attorney's role. Your attorney will be able to advise you of what to expect and how to react to questions from the seller's counsel.

YOUR ATTORNEY

Your attorney will play many roles in your real estate transaction. Your lawyer can provide advice, participate in your offer preparation, represent you in the transaction, and take part in the closing. Your lawyer could be the escrow agent. He can answer all your legal questions and refer you to other professionals for specialized help.

Your attorney will be one of your best friends in the purchase of a home. Lawyers are not cheap, but they are a good value. Your lawyer may be responsible for performing a title search on the property. He can help you with contingencies you should include in your offer. When you have questions regarding real estate law, your attorney is the one to depend on. Brokers should have a broad knowledge of real estate law, but lawyers are your best choice for legal advice.

Brokers are limited in the scope of legal services they may provide. Your broker can fill in the blanks of a real estate contract, but a lawyer can draft the entire document. When you are working with the fine points of law, consult with a reputable real estate attorney. His or her fees will be minimal when compared to the possible results of a poor legal decision. Deed preparation and recording will be done by one of the attorneys. All documents should be reviewed by your attorney before you sign them. In general, don't skimp on attorney fees and lose a bundle based on poor advice. Buying a home is a large enough investment to warrant a top-notch attorney.

THE ESCROW AGENT

The escrow agent is the person or entity holding your earnest-money deposit. This might be one of the attorneys, a real estate broker, or another third party. The escrow agent is responsible for holding and discharging the deposit. If all goes well, the escrow agent will present the deposit at the time of closing. If the deal falls through, he will disperse the funds to the appropriate party. Your dealings with an escrow agent will be minimal.

YOUR LOAN ORIGINATOR

Your dealings with loan originators can produce varied results. There are essentially two types of loan originators. The first type is a salaried employee of the lending institution. The second type earns a commission for every loan they originate

and close. Given a choice, this is the breed of loan officer you want to find. They will be much more liberal and aggressive in getting your loan closed.

If you are working with an experienced real estate broker, she will be able to provide you with several loan officers to talk with. Since brokers normally get paid only if the loan closes, they want the deal to work smoothly. The loan officers they suggest should be willing to work with you. If you are not working with a broker, you will have to identify these brokers on your own.

When you are on your own, finding commissioned loan officers can be difficult. It is not common practice to ask the originators if they work on a commission basis. There are a few subtle ways to scout the territory. When you deal with a commercial bank, you could run into either type of loan officer. Mortgage companies frequently use only commissioned originators. Other types of lenders could be using either type. How should you identify the two types of originators?

One quick test is to ask if the loan officer will meet with you in your home or office. When the originators are willing to meet with you outside the financial institution, there is reason to believe they are working on commission. When you must go into their office, they are probably on the payroll. If the originators give you a pager number or home telephone number, it suggests they work on a commission basis.

The overall service and response from an originator can tip you to his employment situation. If the originator is quick to respond to your call and shows sales skills, you have probably found a commissioned loan officer. If the loan officer doesn't take your call or is slow in returning your call, odds are high that he is a salaried employee. What effect will it make on your loan to work with a commissioned loan originator?

When the originator is paid a commission at closing, he will work hard to close your loan. If your ratios are weak, he may put in extra effort to justify your loan approval. During the loan processing period, he should stay informed of your loan status.

If any minor problems arise, he will be willing to work to solve them. In general, if there is any way for you to obtain financing, a commissioned originator will find it.

A salaried loan officer will not be as motivated to see your loan approved. In fact, salaried loan officers may be very conservative in encouraging your loan approval. If they process too many loans that wind up in default, they could lose their jobs. As salaried employees, they make the same money whether you get a loan or not. Without additional financial reward, they have no reason to stretch their lending criteria. When a commissioned originator uses 28/36 ratios, a salaried loan officer may use 25/33 ratios. By documenting their conservative approach, they have a better defense for their superior if the loan goes bad.

Commissioned loan officers will usually stretch their criteria as far as possible. They have a personal interest in seeing your loan approved. While they cannot break the lender's rules, they can use every angle available. These factors combine to make your success rate more attractive with commissioned originators.

Both types of originators perform the same basic duties. They explain the various financing plans available and pre-qualify prospective loan applicants. They work with loan applicants in completing paperwork to get the loan approval process started. Originators collect loan application fees and provide the borrower with required documentation and disclosures. After loan application is made, they pass the loan package down the line to loan processors. After formal loan application, you may never talk to the originator again. Their job is basically done when the loan package is passed along to the processor.

THE LOAN PROCESSOR

Loan processors are responsible for getting your loan ready to close. When the originator hands them a loan package, they must process the loan. This involves verifying information on your application, requesting a credit report, setting up an appraisal,

and many other duties. This individual can have a tremendous effect on the amount of time needed to close your loan.

As a customer, it is not unreasonable for you to request routine updates from the loan processor. In fact, you may have to turn up the heat on the processor to expedite your loan approval. Many underwriting departments are understaffed and overworked. Most of their customers want their loan closed yesterday. When these customers get frustrated, they call their loan originator. The originator refers them to the loan processor, and the processor is put on the spot.

For a loan processor dealing with dozens of anxious home buyers, you may be just another number. If this is the case, you need to keep yourself abreast of the happenings surrounding your loan approval. Being a daily pest will only result in hard feelings and a slow closing. If you check with the processor on a weekly basis, you should be able to keep your closing on track.

The loan processor prepares all the paperwork necessary for your loan's approval. When he has a complete package, it will be submitted to the deciding powers within the financial institution. In many cases, this is a loan approval board. In some areas, the decision may be left to a single senior loan officer. This is where the buck stops. Your loan's fate will be decided based on the loan processor's package. In most cases, if you have questions about the status of your loan application, you will need to talk to the loan processor.

THE PRIVATE MORTGAGE INSURANCE COMPANY

Private mortgage insurance (PMI) companies have a big say in your loan approval. If they are unwilling to insure your loan, the lender is not likely to approve your financing. Private mortgage insurance is a safeguard for the lender. If you default on the loan, the insurance will protect the lender to an agreed-upon amount. This insurance allows the borrower to obtain a loan with a lower down payment. If you are putting a 20% down payment towards the purchase, PMI will not likely be required.

With a smaller down payment, you will have to pass the scrutiny of the PMI company. If you have good credit and a stable employment history, there should be no problem. If your credit is scarred or you switch jobs frequently, you will be considered a high risk for default. Since the PMI company will have to reimburse the lender if you default on the loan, they can be very picky.

Private mortgage insurance is for the benefit of the financial institution, not the borrower. The only benefit to you is the smaller down payment. Your loan officer will explain the scope of PMI during the application process. It is not an area open for negotiation with most lenders. Generally, if you are putting less than 20% down, you must meet PMI requirements.

If you are dealing with an FHA loan, you will discover MIP. This is a mortgage insurance premium. The role of MIP is essentially the same as that of PMI. In both cases, they provide the lender with some protection against your default on the loan.

THE APPRAISER

The appraiser can make or break your deal. If the appraiser cannot justify the price of your home, the lender's loan amount will be affected. Lenders base their loans on a loan-to-value (LTV) ratio. If you are making a 10% down payment, the lender is loaning 90% of the purchase price. This would be a 90% LTV loan. A lender's percentages will be based on the sale price or the appraised value, whichever is less. The appraised value has much to do with the actual loan amount. Refer to the following example to see how an appraisal can affect your home purchase.

Your contract to purchase has a sale price of $100,000. You have agreed to put a $10,000 down payment towards the purchase of the home. You are seeking a loan for $90,000. You are qualified to borrow $90,000 and your loan is approved, subject to appraisal. The bank has agreed to make you a 90% LTV loan. If the appraised value of the home is $100,000 or more, you don't have any problem. If the house appraises for less than $100,000, you could have a big problem.

Let's say the house only appraises for $92,000. With a 90% LTV loan, the bank will only loan you $82,800. Combining your down payment with the loan will give you $92,800, but the seller wants $100,000. What will you do about the remaining $7,200? If the seller is reasonable, you may be able to renegotiate for a lower price. If he isn't, you will either have to come up with the extra money or pass on the house.

Appraisers provide their reports to protect the lender and to educate the buyer. The appraiser will submit an estimate of value for the proposed property. This estimate is arrived at through several different steps. It normally consists of a cost-to-construct approach and a comparable-sales approach. In each case, the report will show adjustments to make the appraisal fair.

Appraisers are vital elements to financing your new home. You will not have to deal with the appraiser, unless the property does not appraise well. (The seller or his broker will work with the appraiser.) All you have to do is keep your fingers crossed and wait. If there is a problem, you or your broker can provide information to have the appraised value changed. If you can give the appraiser substantiated evidence to increase the appraisal, he will.

THE TITLE SEARCH PROFESSIONAL

In most instances, a title search will be performed by your attorney. This is a process the attorney follows to establish an opinion of title. He will document the chain of the title and any encumbrances on the title. When he has gathered sufficient information, he will render an opinion of title. This title search will protect you and allow the issuance of title insurance.

Title insurance will protect you from most claims against the possession of your property. If a long-lost heir shows up with a dispute of your ownership, title insurance will be very comforting. Title insurance is not required in all states, but it is in your best interest to obtain it. The cost is not prohibitive and the benefits are substantial.

THE HAZARD INSURANCE PROVIDER

If you have tenant's insurance on your possessions, your same insurance agent should be able to provide you with homeowner's insurance. These policies are not very expensive and will be required by your lender. The lender requires the coverage to name them as the first insured. This protects the lender from loss due to fire or other catastrophic losses.

Before you buy hazard insurance, talk with your lender. The lender will be happy to provide you with their minimum requirements for your insurance. For your own protection, you will want more coverage than is required by the lender. The lender will only require coverage against your loan amount. You should purchase insurance with replacement value for your property. This will protect your full investment. Normally, these policies also cover your personal possessions in the home.

THE SURVEYOR

With many transactions, you will need a certified survey. Occasionally, the seller will have a current survey. If he doesn't, you should obtain one. A mortgage survey is the best type to purchase. This will show ground elevations, all structures, and a wealth of other information. This will be more expensive than a boundary survey, but you will be informed as to all aspects of the property.

The value of a mortgage survey can really come into play when there are zoning violations. If the seller built his garage too close to the property line, a mortgage survey will provide enough detail to show the violation. A simple boundary survey will only show the lot lines. Without showing the placement of buildings, you don't know if the property is in compliance with local requirements. Mortgage surveys will also identify properties located in flood zones. The extra cost of a full-blown mortgage survey is a good investment.

THE CODE ENFORCEMENT OFFICERS

As one of your contingencies, you may be in contact with code enforcement officers. This is especially true if you are buying a multi-family property. For the average home purchase, you will not be involved with these professionals. If you are buying an income property, you should request a code enforcement inspection of the property. Many times, small multi-family properties violate code requirements.

If the seller did not obtain the proper code approvals to make a multi-family property, you could be in for a bad surprise. When you purchase the property, you can expect a visit from the tax assessor. If the property is in obvious violation, the tax assessor will notify the code enforcement office. You could be forced to quit using the property as a multi-family building. If you have any reason to suspect code violations, contact the code enforcement office, fast.

ZONING OFFICIALS

Your exposure to zoning officials will be minimal in most residential transactions. Unless you suspect that the property violates local zoning ordinances, you may never talk with these professionals. If you are buying a multi-family property, check with the zoning department. If you wish to operate a home-based business, call the zoning official. Zoning officers are usually easy to get along with and very helpful.

SEPTIC-SYSTEM INSPECTORS

When you purchase a rural property, you will need a septic inspection. These inspectors will come out to the property and investigate the present sewage-disposal system. This is a necessary inspection. You may find the property has an old metal septic tank. When this is the case, it may need to be replaced. This is an expensive job. If the drain-field is not operating properly, the cost to correct the defects could reach several thousand dollars. These inspections will not be expensive, but they should be considered a mandatory expense.

TESTING LABORATORIES

Buying rural property requires a water test. This test will provide information on the quality of your potable water. Since water is essential to life, a good well is essential to your home. The testing lab will provide you with a detailed report on many aspects of your drinking water. A satisfactory water test should be a standard contingency in your purchase offer for properties with private water supplies.

These laboratories may test for many items detrimental to your health. Radon is one of the newer risks commonly tested for. Your broker can advise you on the type of tests frequently conducted in your area. You can also call a few labs and get their opinions on tests you should have done. An experienced real estate attorney will also know what test contingencies should be included in your purchase offer.

PEST-CONTROL PROFESSIONAL

A pest-control professional can keep you from making a big-league mistake. Most pest inspections can be obtained without charge. Pest-control companies typically give free inspections, in hopes of finding a problem. They will look for all types of wood-infesting insects and pests. Wood-borers, powder-post beetles, and termites head the list of their most-wanted villains.

If your intended new home is affected by these creatures, you could be looking at major extermination costs. This is especially true of wood-borers. A tented-fumigation will cost several thousand dollars and is the only sure way to rid the house of these destroyers. Since the inspection will be free or very reasonable, make a pest inspection one of your contingencies. Damage found could make the contract voidable. It would create a negotiable defect that might be paid by either party. Pest inspections are required in some but not all states.

PROFESSIONAL PROPERTY INSPECTOR

In recent years, professional property inspectors have become very popular. Some of these inspec-tors are engineers; others are contractors. They will go through your prospective property with a fine tooth comb to find problems. They might inspect mechanical systems, structural characteristics, and any other possible defect associated with a house.

Inspections can cost a few hundred dollars, but they can save you thousands. If you have an inspection contingency, these inspectors can keep you from buying a lemon. The scope of their inspection may vary, and so will their fees. Shop for your inspector and require verifiable references and credentials. There are some unscrupulous companies afoot. If you are going to pay for a professional inspection, make sure the inspection is done by a qualified company. Real estate brokers and attorneys may be able to refer some trusted names to you. If they can't, rely on references and license credentials. Even if the house you are purchasing is only a few years old, a professional inspection is a good investment.

SPECIALIZED INSPECTORS

While property inspectors may be qualified to inspect all aspects of your property, you may want to take advantage of specialized inspectors. These could include plumbers, electricians, heating companies, roofers, or any other trade. General inspectors are good, but experts are better. No single individual can be expected to be an expert in every trade.

I recommend individual inspections. This may cost a little more, but you are getting opinions from experts in each field. This is a personal choice, and the decision is yours. It makes sense to me to have a plumber look at the plumbing and a structural engineer look at the structure. Contemplate your comfort level and make a decision accordingly. In either case, make provisions in your offer for adequate inspections.

THE CLOSING AGENT

The closing agent could be an attorney, a real estate broker, or a representative of the financial institution. The closing agent will be the person conducting the settlement of your loan and purchase of the property. Your contact with the closing agent will hopefully be a one-time event. If the closing goes smoothly, you will deal with the agent for an hour or so, and then you will own your home.

The closing agent is the person with whom you will have to coordinate your closing date. She is also the individual to whom you will give your evidence of insurance. (Don't forget to bring your insurance binder to the closing!) All funds used for down payment should be in the form of collected funds. This may be a certified check, a cashier's check, or cash. Talk with the closing agent if you have any questions regarding your financial obligations at settlement.

This is the last step to taking title to your new home. After the closing, one of the attorneys will record your new deed and the related paperwork. When you get to this stage, you are a happy homeowner. This is what it is all about. Throughout the closing process, your attorney will be able to answer your questions. If you are working with a broker, the broker will attend the closing. It is a good idea to talk with these professionals before closing, so you will know what to expect. Closing causes great excitement and anxiety. With the proper planning, the settlement will be over in an hour, and you will be a homeowner, not a tenant.

15
Closing the Loan

Leaving the closing table marks the first day of your life as a homeowner. Before you get to the closing, dozens of things may go wrong. Even while you are sitting at the closing table, the entire deal can go up in smoke. It's not over until you own it. There is no time that can be considered safe until the ownership is transferred. While most obstacles will be encountered well before the settlement date, there are ample opportunities for your bubble to burst at the closing.

With some preparation, you can hedge the odds of encountering a bad settlement. Certain events seem to be perennial party poopers. If you identify these threats, you can overcome them. Some of the problems will only delay your closing. Others will kill the deal. As you examine these examples, they may strike you as funny. Can you imagine an escrow agent coming to the closing without the purchaser's earnest-money deposit? If this happens, the closing must be postponed until the deposit is delivered. This seems like something that could only happen in the movies, but I have seen it on more than one occasion. This chapter is filled with thought-provoking events capable of crashing your closing.

THE WRONG LEGAL DESCRIPTION

It is very important to have the proper legal description in your purchase contract. The street address of a property is not sufficient. The *legal* address of the property is best obtained from the property's deed. With newer deeds, the legal address will frequently contain a lot, block, and section number. Older deeds will use a metes and bounds description.

Your contract should contain the legal description as it is described in the deed. Your broker or attorney will be able to provide you with a valid legal description of the property being purchased.

If the legal description is not used or is incorrect, your closing can be affected. At the least, the closing could be postponed. At the worst, you could buy the wrong property. To guard against this type of problem, request a copy of the property's deed. You can get a copy of the deed from the Registry of Deeds. Many real estate brokers will have a copy of the deed in their files. When you have the deed, compare the legal description with the one on your purchase offer. This simple verification can save untold trouble.

TIME IS OF THE ESSENCE

The phrase "Time is of the essence" can work for you or against you. These five words convey power for the person benefiting from them. This phrase is used to make the performance date of a contract urgent. As a purchaser, you might use the phrase to ensure that the seller will convey title by a certain date. A seller can incorporate the language into the contract to require transfer of title no later than the stated settlement date. This is where the clause can have the most detrimental affect on you.

When dealing with a time-is-of-the-essence clause, the closing date becomes critical. If you are unable to close by the agreed-upon date, you could lose your earnest-money deposit. Read your paperwork carefully to determine whether this clause exists. If it does, talk with your attorney before signing the agreement. The legal implications of this clause may vary in different jurisdictions. In most cases, you will want to have the clause removed before signing a contract. If you are working with a contract containing the clause, meeting your closing date is essential. There are very few instances when this phrase is needed. Talk with your attorney about such clauses and avoid them if possible.

TITLE DEFECTS

A clouded title can stop your closing. If the title contains defects, they must be settled before closing. These defects could come in many forms. A common encumbrance is a tax lien. Tax liens are placed against a property when the real estate taxes are delinquent. The past due taxes must be paid when the property is transferred. This obligation can amount to several thousand dollars and may cause your closing to be delayed.

MECHANIC'S LIENS

Mechanic's liens are another common title defect. These liens involve unpaid contractors. If a contractor performs work on a house, he has the right to place a lien against the property if he is not paid. Most title defects turn up in the title search, but mechanic's liens might not. If the seller has just recently had work done on the home, the liens may not have been filed before your title search. Many sellers make improvements to their property before selling it. If the contractors are not paid, they can put a lien on the house.

These liens do not take long to place and can occur after the title search. Since the lien will be against the property, it will affect you, even though you didn't authorize the work. If the lien is discovered before closing, it will be settled before the closing. It may be paid off with the seller's proceeds from the sale at the time of closing. If the lien is not discovered until after closing, you will incur expenses to have it removed.

INDEMNIFICATION

It is a good practice to have your attorney inspect the title the morning before you close the transaction. If a lien was filed since the first title search, this quick inspection will expose it. Your lawyer should be able to provide a clause in your contract to protect you from future liens caused by the seller. Ask your attorney to provide an indemnification clause for this purpose. It will state that the owner has not done anything to give anyone a right to place a lien on the house. If a problem arises, the more paperwork you have signed by the seller, the easier your job will be.

MATERIALMAN'S LIENS

Materialman's liens are similar to mechanic's liens. They protect material suppliers from non-payment. If a company provides building materials for a home and is not paid, the company may file a materialman's lien.

JUDGMENTS

Judgment liens are a result of court-approved action. They are placed to secure a debt owed to someone. If the seller was delinquent in making payments on a loan, the lender might obtain a judgment against the debtor. After going to court, the court might allow the lender to attach a judgment to the seller's property. In extreme cases, the judgment holder may force the sale of the debtor's property.

JUNIOR MORTGAGES

Junior mortgages may be recorded against the property you plan to buy. They must be paid off before you take title. This is normally done during the closing. Second mortgages rarely create a problem. The seller knows they exist and is aware that they must be paid. In the case of other liens, the seller may not be aware of them. When caught by surprise, he may not have the money to clear the title. If this happens, you will have to negotiate a lower price so you can remove the title defects.

INACCURATE CREDIT REPORTS

Mistakes can be made by anyone involved in your transaction, but credit report mistakes can cause you a lot of trouble. Occasionally, inaccurate credit reports are issued to the lender. If this happens, you could be denied your loan, based on the inaccurate information. This stumbling block will be encountered early in the deal. If your lender rejects your loan because of a credit report, request a copy of your credit report from the issuing credit bureau.

When I applied for my first home loan, this unusual problem happened to me. The credit bureau issued a report on someone with the same first and last name as mine, but it wasn't me. This individual had very poor credit and my loan was questioned. After some investigation, we discovered the error. The individual lived on the same street I did and had the same name, except for the middle name. The lender realized something was wrong when the wife's name on the report was not the same as on my loan application. The credit report also showed the individual having several children. At that time, I didn't have any children.

In my case, it was simply a matter of obtaining the proper credit report. My credit was excellent and the loan was approved. If the loan processor had not noticed the discrepancies of the wife's name and the number of children, my loan would probably have been rejected. Sometimes the credit report will be yours, but it will have erroneous information contained in it.

Under these conditions, you will have to work with the credit bureau to clear up the confusion. This can take several weeks. As a preliminary insurance, you may want to obtain a copy of your credit report before making loan application. If you find problems, you can have them corrected without losing time on your closing date.

INSPECTIONS

The home inspection process can reveal many reasons to delay or cancel your closing. If you discover that the well is polluted or that the septic system needs to be replaced, you will not want to follow through with your purchase under the existing terms. Discovering that all the sill plates are rotted is another good reason to put your closing on hold. Any major defect is reason enough to renegotiate your contract with the seller.

If a serious and costly problem is found, you have a few options. If your contract was written well, you can cancel your contract. You could request the seller to correct the defects at his expense. Another option is to renegotiate for a lower sale price. With the right wording in your contingency clause, all options will be open to you.

With any of these choices, your closing may be delayed or canceled. This element is somewhat out of your control. While you have options, the seller must be willing to compromise. Normally, a seller will acknowledge the defects and be willing to work out new terms. While this is frequently the case, you cannot count on it. Some sellers may refuse to lower their price or correct the defects. It could be their hope to find a buyer who will not be as thorough as you have been. This is a problem you cannot prepare for or worry about. You must deal with it when it occurs.

APPRAISALS

A low appraisal can spell instant death for your closing. If you are financing the home, the lender will require an appraisal. These are professional appraisals performed by individuals approved by the lender. If the house you are trying to buy for $108,000 only appraises for $100,000, you have a problem. Lenders base their loan amount on a percentage of the sale price or appraised value, whichever is lower. If the property does not appraise for the amount you have agreed to pay, the lender may deny your loan.

Appraisals are generally requested after you have preliminary loan approval. You must pay for the appraisal, even if it comes in low. If your loan falls through, you lose money. You lose the money you paid for loan application and appraisal fees, perhaps $500 or more. There is no guarantee of what the property will appraise for, but with some research, you can get a good idea of the fair market value.

Before making an offer to purchase the property, create the list of comparable properties. If you are working with a broker, she will do this for you. Ask your broker to perform an in-depth market analysis on the property you plan to buy. She will use the comparable-sales method to develop an opinion of value. You can do this yourself by following the advice given earlier in this book.

By establishing a reasonable estimate of value, you can be more assured that you will not have appraisal problems. If the appraiser has trouble justifying the home's value, provide him with your research information. Establishing what the house is probably worth is a step that should be taken before making an offer. Even with your best efforts, the property may still appraise below the contract price. If this happens, you must look at your options.

If you have extra money, you could pay the difference with a larger down payment. Since most people are unwilling to pay more than the appraised value, you will probably wind up back in negotiations with the seller. With the proper contingency clause, you can void the contract. If you really want the house, ask the seller to accept the appraised value as a sale price. The seller should recognize he is only likely to get an offer based on appraised value from any buyer. If the seller is willing to lower his price, you can move on to the closing. If the seller plays hardball, you must void the contract. In some cases, you might strike a deal in which the two of you split the difference.

A low appraisal is one of the fastest ways to kill a real estate transaction. A preliminary market evaluation will greatly reduce your risks of a low appraisal. If the appraisal is going to stop your closing, it will happen relatively fast. Once you have preliminary loan approval, the appraisal results will be available in a week or two. Before you gamble money you cannot recover, do everything you can to establish the fair market value of the home.

STUPID MISTAKES

Nothing will make your closing more bitter than stupid mistakes. After many years as a professional broker, I have seen closings come to screeching halts for some of the most ridiculous reasons. There are many factors beyond your control that are ca-

pable of killing your closing, but stupid mistakes are not among them. As you read through the following examples, notice how little it takes to ruin your settlement date.

FORGETTING THE EARNEST-MONEY DEPOSIT

When the time comes to close your loan, the lender requires collection of your earnest-money deposit. It is the escrow agent's responsibility to deliver the deposit. I have personally been involved in more than one closing at which the deposit was forgotten. How can a professional escrow agent forget to deliver the deposit? Well, I don't know why they forget, but sometimes they do. Call your escrow agent before the closing and remind him to bring your deposit. The agent may think you are paranoid, but it is better to be safe than sorry.

COLLECTED FUNDS

The closing agent will require all funds to be *collected funds*. This means they will not accept a personal check. The closing agent will require cash or a bank check guaranteed to be good. The agent cannot risk accepting a check that may bounce. In special circumstances, the agent may accept a personal check for some of the closing fees. The closing agent will probably accept a normal check from the escrow agent. To be safe, call the closing agent and ask what amount of money you will need and how it should be delivered. By the day of closing, the closing agent will know the precise amount required to close the deal.

I have seen closings stalled until collected funds could be obtained. Real estate deals can be very volatile. A simple blunder in the type of funds needed for closing costs can delay or inhibit the deal. It may not destroy your transaction, but it can make the whole affair more distasteful. The seller may become outraged by your inability to close. You and the seller may lose time from work without the desired result. Calling the closing agent is a simple solution for avoiding the problem all together.

INSURANCE BLUNDERS

There are three common mistakes made regarding hazard insurance. The first is forgetting to purchase it before closing. The financial institution requires a hazard policy to be in effect before your closing can take place. If you get to the settlement table without your insurance, you may have to postpone the closing. In some cases, the closing agent may allow you to call and arrange for the insurance by telephone.

If you call your insurance agent from the closing and obtain a policy number, the closing agent may allow the closing to continue. While this is worth trying if you forget your insurance, don't count on being allowed this privilege. The closing agent can stop the closing and require it to be rescheduled after your insurance is issued.

Some purchasers buy their hazard insurance but fail to name the lender as the insured. This is another reason for the closing agent to stop your closing. Call the closing agent and ask how your insurance binder should be structured. Confirm the amount of insurance required and how the binder must read. This phone call can save you embarrassment, money, and time.

A third common mistake is forgetting to bring evidence of your insurance to the closing. Some purchasers buy the insurance, have it properly issued, and then forget to bring the binder to closing. A phone confirmation may satisfy the closing agent, but she is not required to close the loan if you don't provide a binder for her closing file. This seems to be one of the most common mistakes made. During the excitement and anxiety of buying a home, it is easy to forget minor details. At first, this may seem like a minor detail, but it can become a major problem at the settlement.

GOING TO CLOSING WITHOUT YOUR SPOUSE

In a majority of closings, both spouses will be required to attend the closing. Today's loans usually require the signatures of both spouses. If you go to the closing alone, you may find the transaction cannot be settled without your spouse's signature. This mistake can be very embarrassing. It can also stop your closing in its tracks. If you plan to attend the closing alone, check with the closing agent first. Make sure your spouse's presence is not required.

CERTIFICATES OF OCCUPANCY

If you are buying a new home, a certificate of occupancy (CO) is required at the closing. This a permit issued by the code enforcement office, deeming the subject property suitable for human habitation. It is the seller's responsibility to provide this certificate, but is in your best interest to check on the status of the certificate. If you are on good terms with the seller, call and remind him to bring the certificate to the closing.

If the builder does not produce a CO, you will not be able to close your loan. Until the CO is issued, it is unlawful to move into the property. With new-home purchases, this is a fairly common obstacle. Builders are anxious to close the deal and overlook the certificate of occupancy. A good closing agent will not look the other way on this issue. If the CO is not available, the loan will not close.

KEYS

If the seller does not bring keys for the property to closing, it may be difficult for you to enjoy possession of the property. This happens more often than you might think. In the haste of getting all the necessary paperwork together, the seller forgets to bring the keys. This is especially true when the seller has not been living in the property. If you are buying a multi-family property, it is a good idea to call and remind the seller to bring all the keys to settlement.

SECURITY DEPOSITS

When you buy a multi-family dwelling, you should receive the tenants' security deposits at closing. As the new owner, you will be responsible for returning these deposits when the tenants move. This is an area often overlooked by everyone. The seller doesn't think of the deposits because he has held them for so long. Many new buyers are unaware that they are supposed to take charge of the deposits. Brokers may forget to remind anyone of the deposits. The closing agent will not be concerned with security deposits; they do not directly affect the closing.

Most purchase contracts address the agreed-upon disposition of security deposits. There are occasions when the closing agent will notice this language and require the deposits to be properly distributed before completing the closing. If this happens, the closing may have to be delayed until the seller can produce the security deposits. If you are buying a multi-family dwelling, call before the closing to remind the seller of the security deposits.

SURVEY PROBLEMS

Before you go to closing, inspect the survey of your intended new property. Sometimes surveys cause big problems. Property lines and appurtenances are not always where they seem to be. I nearly lost a closing from one of my customers over a survey.

My customer was buying a four-unit building as an investment. We had inspected the property and everything seemed fine. When we all sat down at the closing table, the listing real estate broker threw a curve at us. She produced the survey and commenced explaining a little problem she had discovered. When the seller's broker originally showed us the property, she pointed out the property's boundary. Within this boundary was a very nice paved parking area. This building was in a city where parking was a premium asset.

My customer agreed to buy the property, based on representations made by the seller's broker. At the time, there was no survey available on the property. When I prepared my customer's purchase offer, I placed a contingency in the offer requiring a satisfactory survey. Up until the day of closing, this survey was never produced. Then, at the closing table, the seller's broker showed us the survey.

Much of the paved parking area was not a part of this parcel of land. It belonged to a different owner. My customer was shocked and did not know what to do. I asked for a fifteen minute recess from the closing and went into the hall with my customer. He asked my opinion on what he should do. I explained he had the right to void the contract because of the contingency clause I had included. I further told him he had some other options.

One was to accept the property with the loss of much of the parking area. Another option was to renegotiate with the seller for a lower price or different terms. After discussing various aspects of the situation, we met with the seller and his broker. I spoke with both the seller and his broker about their misrepresentation of the property to my customer. They were apologetic and offered to try to make matters right.

After some negotiations, my customer agreed to buy the property, but with different terms. This problem cost my customer some parking space, but won him some attractive owner financing. This deal worked out all right for everyone. No one was sued for misrepresentation, the seller got his sale, the purchaser received his income property with great terms, and the deal closed with less than a two-hour delay.

Under other circumstances, the deal might have died on the spot. Inspect your survey before attending the closing. Check it closely for any defects or misconceptions. If you discover a conflict in the survey, it is easier to solve it before the closing than during it.

ABSENT-MINDED ATTORNEYS

It won't happen often, but every once in a while, an attorney will forget to attend a closing. If you show up planning to close your transaction and your lawyer doesn't, you may have to postpone the settlement. If would be unwise for you to proceed with the settlement in the absence of your lawyer.

I have only seen this happen twice in my career, but both occasions were embarrassing for the purchaser. In one case, the closing was rescheduled for the following week. With the other one, the closing was held later the same day. Lawyers are human and are capable of making mistakes. To be sure you are represented at closing, call your lawyer to confirm the time of your closing. This way, you are sure the lawyer is aware of the closing without insulting him. He thinks you are just anxious and never assumes you are calling to check up on him.

WATER-QUALITY TESTS

If your new property receives its water from a well, you will probably need an approved water test before closing. These tests are often mentioned in purchase agreements, but the results are not always available at the time of closing. In some cases, the test has never been done. In others, someone, usually the broker, neglected to bring the test results to the closing. In many states, the lack of an approved water test will stop the settlement procedures.

This is a simple and inexpensive item capable of ruining everyone's day. Before closing, make sure the responsible individual has satisfactory test results to submit at the closing. It is not unusual for a second test to be required to obtain passing results. Don't wait until the last minute to have the water tested. This should be done well before your scheduled closing date.

PRE-CLOSING TOUR OF THE PROPERTY

Most buyers never inspect the property after it is placed under contract and all contingencies are removed. They go to closing and take title to a property they have not seen for several weeks. A lot can happen in a month to destroy a property. This risk is amplified if the property contains rental tenants.

Average real estate contracts have a clause stating the seller shall convey the property in a condition similar to that as inspected on the date a contract was entered into. The clause allows for regular wear and tear. A majority of real estate transactions close without the property's condition being a problem. It is the minority of real estate deals you must guard

against. Once papers are signed at the closing, you own the property. The closing process is not reversible. There is no recession period for you to change your mind or get your money back. You should inspect the property shortly before your closing date.

Chances are, the property will be fine, but if it isn't, at least you don't own it yet. Imagine your grief if after closing you go to your new home and find it in ruins. If the damage is substantial, you could attempt to sue the seller, but this would take time and money. The simple solution is to inspect the property before the closing. Make sure it is in an acceptable condition and that everything still works.

It only takes a matter of minutes for a heating system to die. One cold night is all it takes to demolish the water distribution pipes in the plumbing. The list of potential problems is too long to mention, but be advised, it does not take long for many costly expenses to crop up. If you inspect the property a day before closing, you can establish the property's current condition.

If you find the property wrecked, it is much easier to deal with it before closing than after. If the water heater is dead, you can lean on the seller to pay for a new one before taking title. If he refuses, you should have grounds to abort the closing. Not many sellers are willing to walk away from a closing for a few hundred dollars. On the other hand, if you have closed on the house *before* discovering the faulty water heater, the problem is yours. Even if you could sue the seller, and it is questionable that you could, the cost of legal action outweighs the cost of a new water heater. With mechanical equipment, it can be very difficult to determine when it stops working.

Legally, you own the property when the closing is complete. How would you prove the water heater broke before the closing? It could have become defective after you signed the papers. Since you didn't discover it until you owned the property, you would be hard pressed to bring any meaningful action against the seller. Take an hour to reinspect your new property before the closing. This simple piece of advice can save you thousands of dollars.

Much of this chapter may seem silly to you. You may buy several properties and never encounter any of these problems. If that is the case, you are lucky. Professional brokers attend dozens of closings each year. We see every imaginable problem related to real estate closings. The examples in this chapter are not meant as entertainment. They have the potential to be serious problems, capable of stopping your closing. When you get so close to home ownership, you don't want a silly circumstance to kill your deal. Read and heed this advice; it may save the day when your turn comes for a closing.

Glossary of Real Estate Terms

ABSTRACT OF TITLE — A summary of all events, recordings, and instruments affecting the title to a property.

ACCELERATION CLAUSE — See DUE-ON-SALE CLAUSE.

ACCRUED INTEREST — Earned, but unpaid interest. Example: A loan is designed to have accrued interest, to be paid at maturity. Interest builds throughout the term of the loan and is paid in a lump sum on the date the loan becomes due in full.

ACQUISITION COST — The sale price and all associated fees incurred to obtain a property.

ACRE — A measurement of land equal to 43,560 square feet.

ADDENDUM — A document added or attached to a contract, becoming a part of the contract.

ADJUSTABLE RATE MORTGAGE (ARM) — A mortgage loan allowing the interest rate to change at specific intervals for a determined period of time.

AMENITIES — In appraisal terms, amenities are benefits derived from property ownership without a monetary value.

AMORTIZATION — The act of repaying a debt gradually in periodic installments.

AMORTIZATION SCHEDULE — A table identifying periodic payment amounts for principal and interest requirements. The table may show the unpaid balance of the loan being profiled.

ANNUAL DEBT SERVICE — The amount of principal and interest required to be paid for a loan.

ANNUAL PERCENTAGE RATE — The effective rate of interest charged over the year for a loan. Note: When discount points are paid, they increase the note rate of a loan to a higher annual percentage rate.

APARTMENT — A residential dwelling contained in a multi-family building, usually rented to a tenant.

APARTMENT BUILDING — A property containing multiple residential dwellings with a common entrance and hallway.

APPRAISAL — An estimated value of a property.

APPRAISER — A person qualified to estimate a property's value.

APPURTENANCE — An item outside the property but considered a part of the realty.

ARM'S LENGTH TRANSACTION — A transaction between parties seeking their personal best interest. Not a transaction between husband and wife, parent and child, or corporate divisions.

AS IS — A term meaning the property is accepted in its present condition, with no warranty or guarantee.

ASKING PRICE — The listed sale price of a property.

ASSESSED VALUE — A value established by an assessor for property tax purposes.

ASSESSMENT — The amount of tax charged by a municipality or local authority for property tax.

ASSESSMENT RATIO — A formula used to determine a property's assessed value, based on the property's market value. Example: If the assessment ratio is 50% and a property has a market value of $100,000, the assessed value of the property is $50,000.

ASSESSOR — An individual who is responsible for determining the assessed value of real property.

ASSIGNEE — A person or an entity to whom a contract is sold or transferred.

ASSIGNMENT — A method used to transfer rights or interest in a contract to another party.

ASSIGNOR — A person or an entity who assigns rights or a contractual interest to another party.

ASSUMABLE MORTGAGE — A mortgage loan that may be assumed from the present mortgagor by another party. Note: When a mortgage is assumed, the person assuming the mortgage accepts responsibility for the debt, but the seller of the property is responsible for the loan if the new buyer defaults on the loan. The seller can be relieved of liability if the lender will grant a novation.

ATTACHMENT — A legal act to seize property to secure or force payment of a debt.

ATTORNEY-IN-FACT — A person or an entity authorized to act for another in the capacity of a power of attorney. The authorization may be limited to certain aspects, or it may be general in scope, with all aspects included.

BACKUP CONTRACT — A binding real estate contract that becomes effective when a prior contract is void.

BALANCE SHEET — A financial sheet showing assets, equity, and liabilities in two columns where the totals of each column balance.

BALLOON MORTGAGE — A mortgage loan with a balloon payment.

BALLOON PAYMENT — A lump sum loan payment due at a specific time.

BANKRUPTCY — A court action to protect debtors who have become insolvent.

BILATERAL CONTRACT — A contractual agreement requiring both parties of the contract to promise performance.

BLANKET MORTGAGE — A mortgage covering more than one real property.

BLENDED RATE LOAN — A loan mixing the interest rate of an existing loan with the current market interest rate to arrive at an attractive interest rate for the blended rate loan.

BLIND POOL — A term used to describe a group of investors placing funds in a program to buy unknown properties.

BROKER — A state-licensed individual acting in the behalf of others for a fee.

BROKERAGE — A business utilizing brokers.

BUILDING CODES — Rules and regulations adopted by the local jurisdiction to maintain an established minimum level of consistency in building practices.

BUILDING PERMIT — A license to build.

CASH FLOW — Term used to describe the amount of money received during the life of an investment.

CERTIFICATE OF INSURANCE — Evidence from an insurer proving the type and amount of coverage on the insured.

CERTIFICATE OF OCCUPANCY — A certificate issued by the code enforcement office allowing a property to be occupied.

CERTIFICATE OF TITLE — An opinion of title provided by an attorney to address the status of a property's title, based on recorded public records.

CHAIN OF TITLE — The history of all acts affecting the title of a property.

CHATTEL — Personal property. Example: A range and refrigerator may be found in a house, but they are chattel, or personal property, not real property.

CHATTEL MORTGAGE — A mortgage loan secured by personal property. Example: An investor buying a furnished apartment building might pledge the furniture as a chattel mortgage.

CLEAR TITLE — A title free of clouds, or liens, that may be considered marketable.

CLOSING — The procedure in which real property is transferred from seller to buyer, and the time when the change of ownership is official.

CLOSING COSTS — Fees incurred during the closing of a real estate transaction. These fees include such items as commissions, discount points, and legal fees.

CLOSING STATEMENT — A sheet detailing a full accounting of all sources and uses of funds in a real estate transaction.

CLOUD OF TITLE — A dispute, an encumbrance, or a pending lawsuit, which, if valid or perfected, will affect the value of the title.

COLLATERAL — Property or goods pledged to secure a loan.

COMMON AREA — The area of a property used by all tenants or owners. Example: hallways and parking areas.

CONSIDERATION — An object of value given when entering into a contract. Examples: earnest money deposit, love and affection, a promise for a promise.

CONTRACTOR — A person or an entity contracting to provide goods or services for an agreed-upon fee.

CONVEY — To transfer to another.

CONVEYANCE — The act of conveying rights or a deed to another.

COUNTER OFFER — A rebuttal offer to a previous offer to purchase real property.

COVENANTS — Promises or rules written into deeds or placed on public record to require or prohibit certain items or acts. Example: a deed may have covenants preventing the use of a home for business purposes.

CREATIVE FINANCING — Any financing deviating from traditional term mortgages.

DEED — A properly signed and delivered written instrument conveying title to real property.

DEED IN LIEU OF FORECLOSURE — The voluntary return of a property to the lender without requiring the foreclosure process.

DEED RESTRICTION — Similar to a covenant, a restriction placed in a property's deed.

DEFAULT — Breaching agreed-upon terms.

DEFECT OF TITLE — A recorded encumbrance prohibiting the transfer of a free and clear title.

DEFERRED PAYMENT — Payments to be made at a later date.

DEFICIENCY JUDGMENT — A court action requiring a debtor to repay the difference between a defaulted debt and the value of the security pledged to the debt.

DEMOGRAPHIC STUDY — Research to establish characteristics of the population of an area, such as sex, age, size of families, and occupations.

DEPOSIT OF EARNEST MONEY — Money placed with an offer to purchase real estate to assure good faith and performance of the contract.

DISCOUNT POINTS — Fees paid to a lender at the time of loan origination to offset the difference between the note rate of the loan and the true annual percentage rate.

DISCRIMINATION — Showing special treatment (good or bad) to an individual based on the person's race, religion, or sex.

DOWN PAYMENT — Money paid as equity and security to cover the amount of purchase not financed.

DRAW — An advance of money from a construction loan to reimburse the contractor for labor and materials put in place.

DUE-ON-SALE CLAUSE — A clause found in modern loans forbidding the owner from financing the sale of the property until the existing loan is paid in full. These clauses can be triggered by some lease-purchase agreements. The clause gives a lender the right to demand the existing mortgage be paid in full, upon demand. Failure to comply can result in the loss of the property to the lender.

DUPLEX — A residential property housing two residential dwellings.

DWELLING — A place of residency in a residential property.

EARNEST MONEY — Money placed with an offer to purchase real estate to assure good faith and performance of the contract.

EASEMENT — A license, a right, a privilege, or an interest that one party has in another party's property.

EQUITABLE TITLE — An interest held by the purchaser of a property placed under contract but not yet closed upon.

EQUITY — The difference between the market value of a property and the outstanding liens against it.

ESCROW — The act of placing certain money or documents in the hands of a neutral third party for safekeeping until the transaction can be completed.

ESCROW AGENT — A person or an entity receiving escrows for deposit and disbursement.

ESTATE FOR LIFE — An interest in real property that ends with the death of a particular person.

ESTOPPEL CERTIFICATE — A document proving the amount of lien or mortgage levied against a property.

EVICTION — A legal method for a property owner to regain possession of real property.

FAIR MARKET RENT — The amount of money a rental property may command in the present economy.

FAIR MARKET VALUE — The amount of money a property may be sold for in the present economy.

FEASIBILITY STUDY — A study used to determine whether a venture is viable.

FIRST MORTGAGE — A mortgage with priority over all other mortgages as a lien.

HYPOTHECATE — The act of pledging an item as security without relinquishing possession of the item.

INCOME PROPERTY — Real property generating rental income.

INSURABLE TITLE — A title to property that is capable of being insured by a title insurance company.

INTEREST-ONLY LOAN — A loan with terms requiring only the payment of interest at regular intervals until the note reaches maturity.

LANDLORD — A person who leases property to another.

LEASEHOLD — The interest a tenant holds in rental property.

LESSEE — A person renting property from a landlord.

LESSOR — A landlord renting property to a tenant.

LETTER OF CREDIT — A document acknowledging a lender's promise to provide credit for a customer.

LEVERAGE — The act of using borrowed money to increase buying power.

LIEN — A notice against property to secure a debt or other financial obligations.

LIFE ESTATE — An interest in real property that terminates upon the death of the holder or other designated individual.

LIFE TENANT — An individual allowed to use a property until the death of a designated individual.

LIMITED PARTNERSHIP — A partnership in which there is a general partner and limited partners. The limited partners are limited in their risk of liability.

LINE OF CREDIT — An agreement from a lender to loan a specified sum of money upon demand without further loan application.

MAI — An appraisal designation meaning "Member, Appraisal Institute."

MARKETABLE TITLE — A title to real property free from defects and enforceable by a court decision.

MORTGAGE BANKER — Someone who originates, sells, and services mortgage loans.

MORTGAGE BROKER — Someone who arranges financing for a fee.

MORTGAGEE — An entity holding a lien against real property.

MORTGAGOR — An entity pledging property as security for a loan.

NET INCOME — The amount of money remaining after all expenses are paid.

NET WORTH — The amount of equity remaining when all liabilities are subtracted from all assets.

NET YIELD — The return on an investment after all fees and expenses of the deal are subtracted.

NOVATION — An agreement in which one individual is released from an obligation through the substitution of another party.

PASSIVE INVESTOR — An investor who provides money but no personal services in a business endeavor.

POINTS — See DISCOUNT POINTS.

PRO-FORMA STATEMENT — A spreadsheet projecting the outcome of an investment.

SECONDARY MORTGAGE MARKET — A system in which mortgages are bought and sold by investors.

WARRANTY DEED — A deed in which the grantor protects the grantee against any and all claims.

ZONING — The legal regulation of the use of private land.

Appendix
Real Estate Forms

HOUSE EVALUATION FORM

ITEM	POOR	FAIR	GOOD	EXCELLENT
Foyer	❑	❑	❑	❑
Hall	❑	❑	❑	❑
Kitchen	❑	❑	❑	❑
Living Room	❑	❑	❑	❑
Dining Room	❑	❑	❑	❑
Family Room	❑	❑	❑	❑
Master Bedroom	❑	❑	❑	❑
Bedroom 2	❑	❑	❑	❑
Bedroom 3	❑	❑	❑	❑
Bedroom 4	❑	❑	❑	❑
Bedroom 5	❑	❑	❑	❑
Master Bathroom	❑	❑	❑	❑
Bathroom 2	❑	❑	❑	❑
Bathroom 3	❑	❑	❑	❑
Half Bath	❑	❑	❑	❑
Closet Space	❑	❑	❑	❑
Floor Coverings	❑	❑	❑	❑
Interior Paint	❑	❑	❑	❑
Plumbing System	❑	❑	❑	❑
Heating System	❑	❑	❑	❑
Electrical System	❑	❑	❑	❑
Basement	❑	❑	❑	❑
Attic	❑	❑	❑	❑
Insulation	❑	❑	❑	❑
Garage	❑	❑	❑	❑
Deck	❑	❑	❑	❑
Siding	❑	❑	❑	❑
Exterior Paint	❑	❑	❑	❑
Lawn	❑	❑	❑	❑
Roof	❑	❑	❑	❑

COMMENTS:

LAND EVALUATION FORM

Property address _____

Legal description _____

_____

Lot dimensions _____

Zoning _____

Road frontage _____

Shape _____

View _____

Land area in square feet _____

Topography _____

Hazards _____

Landscaping _____

Deed restrictions _____

Drainage _____

Easements _____

Improvements _____

Water frontage _____

Wooded or open land _____

Accessibility _____

Land's best points _____

Land's worst points _____

Comments _____

_____

_____

_____

LEGAL DESCRIPTION

ADDRESS _____

MAP _____

BLOCK_____

DEED BOOK_____ PAGE # _____

LOCATION INFORMATION FORM

Property address _____

Legal description_____

_____

Lot dimensions _____

Zoning_____

Road frontage _____

Shape _____

View _____

Land area in square feet _____

Topography_____

Hazards _____

Landscaping _____

Deed restrictions _____

Drainage _____

Easements _____

Improvements _____

_____

UTILITIES

Public water yes/no _____   Public sewer yes/no _____   Electricity yes/no _____

Gas service yes/no _____   Cable TV yes/no _____   Telephone yes/no _____

COMMENTS:

BROKER INVITATION

Please be advised I am selling my property located at_____
_____. I have enclosed a property description and photo for your review. I do not wish to list my property with a real estate agency, but I will be happy to allow you to show the property. I will agree to an open listing for each showing you arrange. If you produce a purchaser, who buys the property, I will pay a sales commission of _____% of the closed sale price. The commission will be paid to your firm at the time of settlement.

To arrange a showing, you must provide _____ hours' notice, prior to the showing. If you have any questions, or wish to arrange a showing, please contact:

_____

(NAME)

_____

(ADDRESS AND PHONE NUMBER)

NOTICE: I DO NOT WISH TO LIST MY PROPERTY, EXCEPT AS AN OPEN LISTING.

BROKER SELECTION LOG

NAME	PHONE	POOR	FAIR	GOOD	GREAT
_____	_____	❑	❑	❑	❑
_____	_____	❑	❑	❑	❑
_____	_____	❑	❑	❑	❑
_____	_____	❑	❑	❑	❑
_____	_____	❑	❑	❑	❑
_____	_____	❑	❑	❑	❑
_____	_____	❑	❑	❑	❑
_____	_____	❑	❑	❑	❑

BROKER COMMISSION ARRANGEMENT

If_____ , broker of the

_____ agency, procures an acceptable offer for the

purchase of my real estate, commonly known as _____, and the
property is successfully sold, the real estate agency shall receive a commission equal to _____%
of the closed sale price. The listed price of this property is _____

_____ ($_____). This commission

agreement will remain in effect from _____ to _____

_____. Seller agrees that if the property is sold within six months to
anyone the broker has registered with the seller, as a prospective buyer, the broker shall be entitled to
the above commission. This does not apply if the seller lists the property with a licensed real estate
brokerage on an exclusive basis.

_____   _____
SELLER   DATE   BROKER   DATE

_____
SELLER   DATE

CONTRACT FOR SALE OF REAL ESTATE

Contract made this _____ day of _____, 19____, at _____,
State of _____, by and between _____ (Seller)
and _____ (Purchaser). Seller hereby agrees to
sell, and Purchaser hereby agrees to purchase, a certain lot or parcel of land with any building or
improvements thereon (premises) situated in _____, State of _____, and
described as follows:

_____

The following items to be included in this sale:

_____

_____

Said premises shall be conveyed within _____ days from the date of this contract by a good and
sufficient _____ deed or seller conveying good and merchantable title to the same, free from all
encumbrances, except existing easements, restrictions, conditions, and covenants of record, existing
building and zoning laws, and usual and customary public utility easements servicing the premises;
however, should the title prove defective, then the Seller shall have a reasonable time after due notice
of such defect or defects to remedy the title, after which time, if such defect or defects are not corrected
so that there is a merchantable title, then the Purchaser may at his option, be relieved from all obligations
hereunder and withdraw earnest money or deposits, if any. And for such deed and conveyance purchaser
shall pay the sum of _____ dollars ($_____),
payment to be made as follows:

1. $_____ received of Purchaser as earnest money in part payment on account for
said lot or parcel of land with any buildings or improvements thereon and items included, if any. That

_____ shall hold said earnest money or deposit and act as escrow
agent until transfer of title; that _____ days will be given for obtaining the Seller's
acceptance; and in the event of the Seller's non-acceptance, this earnest money shall be promptly
returned to Purchaser.

2. $_____ to be paid at the time of delivery of the transfer deed in cash, or by
certified, cashier's, bank, or treasurer's check.

3. For a total purchase price of _____

($_____).

This contract is subject to the following conditions:

_____

Full possession of said premises shall be delivered to Purchaser at the time of the delivery of the transfer
deed, said premises to be then in the same condition in which they now are, except in the case of new
construction. New construction shall be completed according to attached plans and specifications and
approved for occupancy by the local code enforcement officials. Reasonable use and wear of the
buildings thereon are the only exception for existing buildings. The following items will be prorated
as of the date of the transfer of said deed:

CONTRACT FOR SALE OF REAL ESTATE

Utilities, fuel, rents, real estate taxes for the current taxing period, for the town/city/county of

_____

The risk of loss or damage to said premises by fire or otherwise until the transfer of title hereunder is assumed by the Seller.

All covenants and agreements herein contained shall extend and be obligatory upon the heirs, personal representatives, and assigns of the respective parties. That in case of failure of purchaser to make either of the payments, or any part thereof, or to perform any of the covenants on its part made or entered into, this contract shall, at the option of the Seller, be terminated and Purchaser shall forfeit said earnest money; and the same shall be retained by Seller as liquidated damages and the escrow agent is hereby authorized by Purchaser to pay over to Seller the earnest money, if any.

This contract is also subject to a satisfactory water test, by a testing service approved by the State of

_____

The results of said inspection must be conveyed to all parties within _____ days of the final acceptance of this contract. Cost of this test to be paid by _____.

If a broker is involved, Purchaser acknowledges that _____ represents the Seller and Seller acknowledges that _____ represents the Purchaser.

Witness our hands and seals on the day and year first above written.

I/we hereby agree to purchase the above described premises at the price and upon the terms and conditions above set forth.

| _____ | | _____ | |
| WITNESS | DATE | PURCHASER | DATE |

| _____ | | _____ | |
| WITNESS | DATE | PURCHASER | DATE |

I/we hereby accept the offer and agree to deliver the above described premises at the price and upon the terms and conditions above set forth.

I/we further agree to pay a commission for services herein of _____ percent of the sale price to the listing brokerage.

| _____ | | _____ | |
| WITNESS | DATE | PURCHASER | DATE |

| _____ | | _____ | |
| WITNESS | DATE | PURCHASER | DATE |

CONTRACT EXTENSION

The time for performance of the purchase and sale agreement dated _____, between

_____, Purchaser, and

_____, Seller, for the sale of the real estate commonly

known as _____,

is hereby extended until _____.

Witness our hands and seals this _____ day of _____, 19_____.

_____   _____
PURCHASER   SELLER

_____   _____
PURCHASER   SELLER

CONTINGENCY PURCHASE CLAUSE

This contingency purchase clause shall become an integral part of the purchase and sale agreement

dated _____, between _____,

Purchasers, and _____, Sellers, of the real prop-

erty commonly known as _____. The Sellers
retain the right to continue to market their property for sale and to accept offers subject to the rights of
the Purchasers in this agreement. Sellers may accept such an offer, subject to Purchasers' rights and after
giving Purchasers 72 hours from the time of notification to remove this contingency and agree to a
definite settlement date with the Sellers. If the Purchasers cannot perform to these specifications, the
Sellers may void the contract, return all deposit money held for Purchaser, and sell the property to
another party. In the event the need for notification arises, the Purchasers may be notified by certified

return receipt mail at _____, and

the Sellers may be notified at _____. The date indicated on the
return receipt as the day of receipt shall be the date of notification.

_____   _____
PURCHASER   DATE   SELLER   DATE

_____   _____
PURCHASER   DATE   SELLER   DATE

CONTINGENCY RELEASE

This contingency release shall become an integral part of the purchase and sale agreement dated

_____, between _____, Purchasers,

and _____, Sellers, of the real property commonly known as

_____.

The following contingencies are hereby removed from the above mentioned contract:

_____

_____

_____

| PURCHASER | DATE | SELLER | DATE |

| PURCHASER | DATE | SELLER | DATE |

ADDENDUM

This addendum is an integral part of the purchase and sale agreement dated _____,

between the Purchasers,_____,and

the Sellers, _____, for the real estate

commonly known as _____. The undersigned parties hereby agree
to the following:

_____

_____

_____

_____

| PURCHASER | DATE | SELLER | DATE |

| PURCHASER | DATE | SELLER | DATE |

INSPECTION ADDENDUM

This addendum shall become an integral part of the purchase and sale agreement dated

_____, between _____, Purchasers,

and _____, Sellers, of the real property commonly

known as _____. Within _____ days of acceptance of the

above mentioned contract the Purchasers shall order an inspection of the property located at

_____, from a qualified representative of the Purchasers' choice at the Purchasers' own expense. This inspection shall include the items indicated and checked below:

❏	Roof	❏	Appliances
❏	Heating system	❏	Chimney
❏	Cooling system	❏	Septic
❏	Foundation	❏	Well
❏	Plumbing	❏	Code violations
❏	Electrical	❏	Drainage systems
❏	Other _____		

In the event the Purchasers are not satisfied with the inspection results, they may void this contract if written notice is given to the Sellers by _____. Sellers agree to allow reasonable access to the property for the purpose of this inspection. Additional terms and conditions are as follows:

_____   _____
PURCHASER   DATE   SELLER   DATE

_____   _____
PURCHASER   DATE   SELLER   DATE

DISCLOSURE ADDENDUM

This addendum is an integral part of the property disclosure form dated _____ , by the
Sellers of the real estate commonly known as _____ .
The undersigned parties hereby disclose the following:

_____

_____

_____

_____

_____

_____

_____

_____

_____

_____

_____

_____

_____

SELLER	DATE	PURCHASER	DATE

SELLER	DATE	PURCHASER	DATE

BROKER   DATE

FHA ADDENDUM

This addendum is an integral part of the purchase and sale agreement dated _____ , between the Purchasers, _____ , and the Sellers, _____ , for the sale of the real estate commonly known as _____ .

It is expressly agreed that, notwithstanding any other provisions of this contract, the Purchasers shall not be obligated to complete the purchase of the property described herein or to incur any penalty by forfeiture of earnest-money deposits or otherwise, unless the Sellers have delivered to the purchaser a written statement issued by the Federal Housing Commissioner, setting forth the appraised value of the property for mortgage insurance purposes of not less than $_____ _____($_____), which statement the Sellers hereby agree to deliver to the Purchasers promptly after such appraised value statement is made available to the seller. The Purchasers shall, however, have the privilege and option of proceeding with the consummation of this contract without regard to the amount of the appraised valuation made by the Federal Housing Commissioner.

_____	_____	_____	_____
PURCHASER	DATE	SELLER	DATE
_____	_____	_____	_____
PURCHASER	DATE	SELLER	DATE

VA ADDENDUM

This addendum is an integral part of the purchase and sale agreement dated _____ , between the Purchasers, _____ , and the Sellers, _____ , for the sale of the real estate commonly known as _____ .

It is expressly agreed that, notwithstanding any other provisions of this contract, the Purchasers shall not incur any penalty by forfeiture of earnest money or otherwise be obligated to complete the purchase of the property described herein, if the contract purchase price or cost exceeds the reasonable value of the property established by the Veterans Administration. The Purchasers shall, however, have the privilege and option of proceeding with the consummation of this contract without regard to the amount of the reasonable value established by the Veterans Administration.

_____	_____	_____	_____
PURCHASER	DATE	SELLER	DATE
_____	_____	_____	_____
PURCHASER	DATE	SELLER	DATE

CONTRACT RELEASE

We hereby agree that the contract of sale dated _____ between

_____, Sellers, and

_____, Purchasers, is null and void. Purchasers and Sellers shall have no rights, claims, or liabilities thereunder and each of them specifically waives any claims or rights he may have against any of the others. We further authorize _____

_____ to release earnest money deposited to the

Purchasers in the amount of _____, ($_____).

_____		_____	
SELLER	DATE	PURCHASER	DATE
_____		_____	
SELLER	DATE	PURCHASER	DATE
_____		_____	
BROKER	DATE	BROKER	DATE

COUNTER OFFER

This counter offer is in response to the purchase and sale agreement dated _____,

between the Purchasers, _____, and the Sellers,

_____, for the sale of the real estate commonly known as

_____.

All other terms shall remain the same, Sellers retain the right to accept any other offer prior to written acceptance and delivery of this counter offer back to the Sellers. This counter offer shall expire at

_____ o'clock AM/PM on _____, unless an executed, accepted copy is returned to the Sellers, prior to the above deadline. The following counter offer is submitted for your review:

_____

_____

_____

_____		_____	
SELLER	DATE	PURCHASER	DATE
_____		_____	
SELLER	DATE	PURCHASER	DATE

MULTIPLE OFFER NOTIFICATION

In response to your offer to purchase the real estate commonly known as _____ _____, dated _____, please be advised there are multiple offers for the purchase of the property at this time. All of the offers are unacceptable, therefore, new offers are welcome and will be reviewed on _____, at _____ o'clock, AM/PM. New offers will be accepted in person, with an appointment, or by mail. Seller retains the right to accept any offer or to reject all offers.

_____

SELLER   DATE

PURCHASE OPTION

In consideration of the payment by _____, hereinafter referred to as optionee, in the amount of _____ ($_____) receipt of which is hereby acknowledged by _____, optionor, agrees to grant optionee the option to purchase the real estate described as_____ _____, and commonly known as _____, in the city of _____, for a purchase price of _____, ($_____) under the following terms and conditions:

If option is exercised, said option will place into force the purchase and sale agreement signed by all parties dated _____, that contains a contingency allowing this option to purchase prior to the purchase and sale contract being effective.

If not exercised by _____, this option shall expire and optionor shall be released from all obligations from this agreement and from the purchase and sale agreement. Optionee's rights shall cease and the above named consideration shall be retained by the optionor.

Time is of the essence in this agreement.

To exercise this option, the optionee shall deliver written notice to the optionor at the address of _____, prior to the expiration of this option. An additional deposit in the amount of _____($_____) shall be placed with an escrow agent as detailed in the purchase and sale agreement.

If notice is mailed, the date received indicated on the return receipt of the certified mail shall be the date of notification.

_____   _____
OPTIONOR   DATE   OPTIONEE   DATE

_____   _____
OPTIONOR   DATE   OPTIONEE   DATE

EXERCISE OF OPTION

To _____, Optionor, as Optionee, it is my intent to

exercise the option agreement dated _____, between the Purchasers,

_____, and the Sellers,

_____, for the sale of the real estate

commonly known as _____.

The escrow agent for this transaction is:

Name _____

Address _____

Phone _____

The amount deposited in escrow is _____ ($_____) and this

deposit was made on _____.

_____   _____
OPTIONOR   DATE   OPTIONEE   DATE

_____   _____
OPTIONOR   DATE   OPTIONEE   DATE

PURCHASER'S NEEDS FOR LOAN APPLICATION

❑ Home address(es) for the last five years

❑ Child support agreements

❑ Social security number

❑ Two years' tax returns, if self-employed

❑ Paycheck stubs, if available

❑ Employee's tax statements (i.e., W-2, W-4)

❑ Gross income amount of household

❑ All bank account numbers, balances, names, and addresses

❑ All credit card numbers, balances, and monthly payments

❑ Employment history for last four years

❑ Divorce agreements

❑ Information on all stocks or bonds owned

❑ Life insurance face-amount and cash value

❑ Details of all real estate owned

❑ Rental income and expenses of investment property owned

❑ List of credit references with account numbers

❑ Financial statement of net worth, if available

❑ Checkbook for loan application fees

EARNEST MONEY DEPOSIT RECEIPT

This will serve as receipt for the earnest money deposit received of

_____, Purchasers of the real estate commonly known

as _____.

The Sellers of this property, _____, will place this earnest money

on deposit with the following lender _____, of

_____.

Any special arrangements for this deposit will be as follows:

_____

_____

_____

PURCHASER	DATE	SELLER	DATE

PURCHASER	DATE	SELLER	DATE

PURCHASER NOTIFICATION

To Purchaser:

_____ Purchaser _____ Purchaser

In accordance with the contract of sale dated _____, and the contingency-purchase
clause dated _____, between you and _____,
Seller, you are hereby notified of the following:

The Sellers of the property commonly known as _____
have accepted a written offer for the purchase of the above real estate subject to your rights in the
contingency-purchase clause. You are requested to respond within 72 hours by either signing and
returning the enclosed contract release form or providing evidence of your ability to purchase the
property with a settlement date of _____.

Please respond to the Sellers at the following address: _____

_____

SELLER	DATE	SELLER	DATE

SELLER'S DISCLOSURE FORM

Owner _____

Owner's address _____

Property address _____

Age of structure _____

How long has the seller owned the property? _____

WATER SUPPLY INFORMATION

Public yes/no _____ private yes/no_____ drilled/dug/artesian _____

Other (describe) _____

Location _____date installed _____

Installed by whom _____

Have any problems ever been experienced with the following:

Water quality _____quantity _____pump_____

Discoloration _____other _____

Has the water ever been tested?_____yes/no _____date of test _____

Are test results available? yes/no_____

Have any test results ever been unsatisfactory or satisfactory with notation? yes/no if yes,

what steps were taken to remedy the problems _____

WASTE DISPOSAL SYSTEM

Public yes/no_____private yes/no_____quasi-public yes/no _____

Have there been any problems with waste disposal? yes/no _____

If yes, explain: _____

If system is private, circle the appropriate type of system:

septic   leach   holding tank   other

Tank size _____

Tank installation date _____

Type of tank: concrete _____ metal _____ other _____

Tank location _____

Company providing service _____

Have you experienced any malfunctions? yes/no _____

If yes, explain: _____

Does system comply with current code requirements? yes/no_____

If no, explain: _____

Comments: _____

INSULATION

TYPE/AMOUNT	NONE	UNKNOWN
Attic/cap	❑	❑
Walls	❑	❑
Floors	❑	❑
Other	❑	❑

Was insulation installed during your ownership? yes/no _____

If yes, by whom: _____

Comments: _____

HAZARDOUS MATERIALS

Do you have knowledge of current or previously existing known hazardous materials, on or in the property, such as:

Toxic materials	yes _____	no _____	unknown _____
Landfill	yes _____	no _____	unknown _____
Radioactive material	yes _____	no _____	unknown _____
Other	yes _____	no _____	unknown _____

Comments: _____

ASBESTOS

On heating pipes	yes _____	no _____	unknown _____
In siding	yes _____	no _____	unknown _____
In floor coverings	yes _____	no _____	unknown _____
In roof shingles	yes _____	no _____	unknown _____
Other locations	yes _____	no _____	unknown _____

Comments: _____

RADON

Has the property been tested for radon? yes/no

If yes, what types of test were conducted? air/water

Test date _____ Are results available? yes/no

Have any steps been taken to reduce radon? yes/no

Comments: _____

LEAD-BASED PAINT

Does the property contain lead-based paint? yes/no/unknown

Are you aware of any cracking, peeling, or flaking paint? yes/no

Comments: _____

UNDERGROUND STORAGE TANKS

Are there now, or have there ever been, any underground storage tanks on the property? yes/no/unknown

If yes, are tanks in current use? yes/no

What materials are or were stored in the tanks? _____

Age of tanks _____ Size of tanks _____

Location _____

Have you ever experienced any problems such as leakage? yes/no

Are tanks registered with the authorities? yes/no

If tanks are no longer in use, have tanks been abandoned according to the local authority's regulations? yes/no

Additional items of disclosure are provided on the disclosure addendum, if any. Are there any? yes/no

The purchaser is encouraged to seek information from professionals regarding specific issues of concern involving hazardous materials or other concerns arising from this property.

| _____ | _____ | _____ | _____ |
| SELLER | DATE | PURCHASER | DATE |

| _____ | _____ | _____ | _____ |
| SELLER | DATE | PURCHASER | DATE |

| _____ | _____ |
| BROKER | DATE |

PROGRESS CHART

EVENT	SCHEDULED DATE	ACTUAL DATE
Disclosure signed by Purchasers	_____	_____
Contract signed by all parties	_____	_____
Earnest money deposited	_____	_____
Purchaser's inspection	_____	_____
Contingencies removed	_____	_____
Loan application made	_____	_____
Loan sent to underwriting	_____	_____
Loan approval received	_____	_____
Commitment letter issued	_____	_____
Rate and points locked in	_____	_____
Preliminary loan approval	_____	_____
Title work started	_____	_____
Title work completed	_____	_____
Appraisal ordered	_____	_____
On-site appraisal	_____	_____
Appraisal complete	_____	_____
Hazard insurance obtained	_____	_____
Settlement scheduled	_____	_____
Earnest money taken to settlement	_____	_____
Signed closing statement received	_____	_____
Transaction complete	_____	_____

PROGRESS CHART

EVENT	SCHEDULED DATE	ACTUAL DATE

Index